Samuel Irenæus Prime

Fifteen years of prayer in the Fulton Street meeting

Samuel Irenæus Prime

Fifteen years of prayer in the Fulton Street meeting

ISBN/EAN: 9783337283926

Printed in Europe, USA, Canada, Australia, Japan

Cover: Foto ©Lupo / pixelio.de

More available books at **www.hansebooks.com**

FIFTEEN YEARS OF PRAYER.

FIFTEEN YEARS OF PRAYER

IN THE

FULTON STREET MEETING.

BY

S. IRENÆUS PRIME,

AUTHOR OF THE "POWER OF PRAYER," "FIVE YEARS OF PRAYER," ETC.

NEW YORK:
SCRIBNER, ARMSTRONG & CO.
1872.

Entered according to Act of Congress, in the year 1872, by
SCRIBNER, ARMSTRONG & CO.
In the Office of the Librarian of Congress, at Washington.

PREFACE.

Every day, except Sundays, during the last fifteen years a public meeting for prayer has been held at the corner of Fulton Street and William, in the city of New York. The reports of that meeting have been widely published. Their line has gone out into all the earth, and their words unto the end of the world.

In two volumes previously published, the compiler of this has given some condensed account of the results of this meeting. The first volume appeared at the end of the first year. The second embraced the records of the first five years. Fifteen years are now completed, and again the reports are gathered up to the praise of divine grace and a testimony to the faithfulness of God.

The FACTS are given, and the reader may make of them what he will. Those who do not believe that God is, and that He rewards those who diligently seek

Him, may smile incredulously at the simplicity of those who accept these statements as illustrations and proofs of the power of prayer. But to us who believe, these are the records of our own experience and observation. We do not pretend to explain them. They are the historical evidences that men ask the Invisible God for certain things, and the answer comes. Often the precise thing asked for is given. Sometimes it is not. There are conditions not always complied with. But here are scores of cases in which the answer is so obviously related to the request, that we have no doubt as to the fact that prayer was heard. Skepticism may reject the record. But Christianity finds its faith strengthened and its heart cheered by these great truths.

No praying person can read this book without deep emotion and great spiritual benefit. If it is read by chapters in prayer-meetings, the church will be quickened and encouraged. Many revivals of religion in England and France, and other countries, followed the public reading of the former volumes. The compiler hopes that this may be even more useful.

He does not claim to be the author of these pages. They are reports furnished to him, mainly by the Rev. L. G. Bingham, who has been a daily attendant upon the meetings from their commencement, and who has done more than any other one man to bring the fruits of these meetings to the knowledge of the public.

With the earnest prayer that this book may be approved of God, it is dedicated to Christ and the Church.

New York, September 1st, 1872.

CONTENTS.

CHAPTER I.
ORIGIN OF THE MEETING. 13

CHAPTER II.
SPIRIT OF THE MEETING. 20

CHAPTER III.
FULTON STREET 25

CHAPTER IV.
INFLUENCE OF PRAYER ON THE COUNTRY . . 33

CHAPTER V.
INFLUENCE UPON THE WORLD. 39

CHAPTER VI.
REMARKABLE CONVERSIONS 50

CHAPTER VII.
COMING TO THE LIGHT 75

CHAPTER VIII.
Up From the Gates of Death 90

CHAPTER IX.
The Sea Giving Up 108

CHAPTER X.
Parents and Children 123

CHAPTER XI.
Answers to Prayer 135

CHAPTER XII.
Power of Prayer 150

CHAPTER XIII.
Religious Anxieties 167

CHAPTER XIV.
Personal Efforts 184

CHAPTER XV.
The Convert's Hour 200

CHAPTER XVI.
One in Christ Jesus 219

CHAPTER XVII.
Parents and Children 232

CHAPTER XVIII.
Various Operations of the Holy Spirit . . 253

CHAPTER XIX.
Hope for the Intemperate 290

CHAPTER XX.
Growth in Grace 310

CHAPTER XXI.
The Revival of 1872 329

FIFTEEN YEARS OF PRAYER.

CHAPTER I.

Origin of the Meeting.

On the 1st of July, 1857, a man was walking down Fulton Street, in the City of New York (one of the most thronged and busy streets of this great metropolis), whose life from that day was to be devoted, as it had never been before, to works of benevolence in the lower wards of the City. In this street this man had been converted some years before. He had been a clothing merchant for a time in a store near by, but was not successful. He was without family, but had hosts of friends. He was of a genial and kindly disposition; of pleasing address, carrying the marks of Christian benevolence in his face; and past middle life.

He had turned out of Broadway, and as he passed rapidly down Fulton Street he met thousands coming up the same, who had come over from Brooklyn—the great dormitory of New York—in population the third city in the United States. They were going to their places of business, and he was going to his. He had been appointed lay missionary for these lower wards, by the Consistory of the Collegiate Reformed Dutch Church, in connection with the Old North Church, situated at the corner of Fulton and William Streets. This day he was to enter upon his labors, and he was hastening at an early hour to the place which was to be his headquarters. Had his appointment as lay missionary anything to do with the origin of the Fulton Street Prayer Meeting? We shall see.

This man was of an ardent, sympathizing temperament, and was a devoted, earnest Christian. He regarded his duties as lying among the neglected in the midst of a dense population—thousands of whom were going down to death without care or warning. He had accepted his appointment with joy, as giving him something to do for Christ, something for souls ready to perish.

He was a missionary to *them*. He was to visit the poor, the sick, and the dying. He was to persuade the children and the youth to attend upon Sabbath School, to lead the riper in years and sin to attend the House of God on the Sabbath. He was this morning—this first day of July, 1857—stepping into a new and laborious field. He hardly knew much as yet of his duties, but the Lord was directing his steps.

He was an observant man—observant of the habits of the people—and quick to discover the means of doing them good.

In the rear of this North Reformed Dutch Church, then more than a century old, were three halls or rooms, one above the other, fitted up for Sabbath School, Bible Class, and week-day religious services. One day as the missionary was traversing the streets, and thinking of the unthinking multitudes around him, the thought occurred to him: "Why not have a noon prayer-meeting in one of these rooms, to be held every day from 12 M. to 1 P.M., with the understanding that men can come in for 10 or 20 minutes, or the whole hour, as may suit their convenience—coming and going to be considered no interruption? This hour is given up for rest and refreshment by the toilers in business: why not give a portion of it in prayer? It might be so conducted that persons of all denominations should feel at home, and no disputed points of doctrine or practice should be discussed. Prayers could be short and specific—songs of praise short—reading of the Scripture short—remarks short—all adapted to the fleeing hour." It was no sooner thought of, than the resolution was taken, and the first meeting was held Sept. 23d, 1857. The missionary sat out the first half hour alone—in silent prayer. At length footsteps were heard on the stairs leading to the place of prayer, and five more entered—making six in all—representing four denominations of Christians. Thus the Lord set his seal to it, that this should be a Union Prayer Meeting for all time. This was the ordering of God's providence. It was not of man's devising; and it is not to be ignored or overlooked that this union meeting has had a powerful influence in promoting the spirit of unity and concord which now prevails throughout Christendom—holding Christ as the head, and members of his body, and members one of another. But have we yet found the origin of the Fulton Street Prayer Meeting? There was a Power working before all this, and deeper down than all this, out of whose operations this meeting sprung. God was preparing the nation for prayer. The summer and autumn of 1857 was a season of great commercial embarrassment. Men's hearts failed them, for fear of the things which were coming upon them. It seemed to the business community that everything was going to general ruin. There was a great scarcity of money—and business had been done on a scale so bold, that when the financial pressure came, men could not see how they were to stand the strain; and many began to cry to God for help, before the missionary issued his call to prayer. And when he did, it was with no expectation that it would be, what it almost at once became—a crowd filling all the rooms in the rear of the Church. Business men wore anxious and solemn faces. Many were in sore distress—having made shipwreck of their fortunes. Men took counsel of their fears, thinking it high time to look to a Power that is above all human power.

A friend had occasion at this time to go into a large store, and as he ascended to the fourth story, he heard the voice of prayer somewhere—he could not tell where: he opened a door to ascertain whence it came—and there was a boy upon his knees, pleading with God to keep his father from *failing*. The father did not *fail*. At another time, going into a merchant's counting-room, the head man of the place said to him: "Let us kneel and ask God to help me through, for without His help, I shall be a bankrupt before the setting of the sun." So we knelt and prayed. That man went through the pressure, and did not become a bankrupt.

Men were prepared for praying, and no sooner was it noised abroad that they were praying in Fulton Street, than men of all classes, and all forms of religious belief ran together for prayer. All honor to the man who suggested the time and place, though the thoughts of his heart did not conceive of the meeting as it all at once grew to be, and so has continued to be for fifteen years.

CHAPTER II.

The One Great Blessing.—The Request and General Results.

THUS, fifteen years ago, September 23, 1857, in the upper room of the Consistory building, Fulton, near William Street, was held a little unpretending meeting for prayer. In this little assembly of six persons was represented four denominations—the Reformed, the Presbyterian, the Congregationalist, and Baptist. And in the next meeting, one week from this day, came the Methodist and Episcopalian. It was no human contrivance to bring together the representatives of the six leading denominations of the country and of the world. It was not thought of. It was the humble inauguration of a spirit of unity, such as the world had never seen since the Reformation. As yet a daily meeting was not thought of. It was simply to pray together once a week—for what? Not deliverance from temporal distresses and embarrassments; though these were everywhere. But the great errand was to pray for the OUTPOURING OF THE HOLY SPIRIT. This was the *necessity* and the object of *desire*. All felt that this was the greatest blessing they could ask for—as it ever has been and ever will be. And so ready was God to answer prayer that from the first the rain of Heavenly grace began to descend in copious effusions, and the place became filled with the Divine presence as in Pentecostal days. So greatly were these meetings blessed, that it was resolved to hold them every day, from that time and onward. And from the first daily meeting till now, in all these fifteen years, there has never been a day on which a meeting has not been held—except upon the Sabbath. In sunshine and in storm, heat and cold, there have been meetings of wonderful prayer—and not less wonderful now than in the beginning. At the end of the second week was held the third of the series, and from that they have been held daily.

We are particular to mention these facts to show that they are of God and not man. God chose a time to display His mercy and grace when there was great commercial embarrassment, and men's hearts were full of fear. Yet this was not mentioned in prayer, so earnest was the meeting to realize the promise of the Father—that He would pour out His Spirit in answer to prayer.

Multitudes of business men stood on the very verge of ruin over the whole land. Their feet were almost gone; but the meeting was not to pray for salvation from commercial failures.

The third meeting was attended by such large numbers, and was pervaded by such an influence of power that it was then resolved to hold meetings daily from 12 to 1 o'clock. From the very first, the presence of Divine influence was manifest; and great was the company of them who were led of the Spirit to believe in Christ as the Saviour of sinners. Soon a room in the second story of the building had to be opened, and both rooms were crowded.

THE SPIRIT OF THE MEETING.

This was from the first as remarkable as the numbers who came. It was a spirit of humble, simple, fervent, united, believing, prevailing prayer, which characterized every assembly. Tears were seen falling—who could or who would restrain them? It was impossible; but all was still and solemn. There was no noise, no sensational movements or demonstrations. There was a fear of machinery or of human instrumentality to work upon the feelings, and they never appeared. They would have been shocking to the religious sense of the meeting. Men sought to be led of the Spirit, and His presence and power were felt and acknowledged every day with joy and thanksgiving. Men were timid of themselves—they feared to touch the ark of God. And yet they were "strong in the Lord, and in the power of His might."

It was some weeks after the beginning of the meetings when the *first request* for prayer was presented. A man came into the porch of the lower lecture room; this room was packed; every seat full, every inch of standing room occupied. He held up an envelope in his hand, and asked that it might be passed up to the leader's desk. It took its way, over the heads of many, from hand to hand, till it reached the leader's. He soon arose and read as follows:

"A widowed mother of an only son, comes asking you to pray for his *immediate conversion*. He is a child of prayer. His father was a minister of the glorious gospel of the blessed God. This son has been given up to God by a holy consecration to Jesus, which to-day has been renewed. He is no longer in the highest sense mine; but in the highest possible sense he is the Lord's. Oh! dear praying brethren! hear the cry of a mother, and pray that my dear boy may be converted; now in this accepted time—now in this day of salvation! I feel an agony of desire that the son shall stand up in the place of the father to proclaim the unsearchable riches of Christ."

The leader read the request impressively, and it

fell on the meeting as a loud call to faith and prayer. Many eyes were full of tears, and the supplications which followed, by one and another, moved every heart. There seemed to be assurance that the young man was *saved*.

After this, requests began to be numerous, and some looked upon the movement with jealousy, as savoring of human contrivances. Some were fearful of the influences of such proceedings. A speaker said one day: "I am afraid of this. I am afraid of spiritual pride. I am afraid the Holy Spirit will be grieved and leave us. I have my misgivings about these requests for prayer." And he sat down.

Instantly another was on his feet and said: "Oh! do not discourage these requests for prayer. Let them come, and let us pray for all for whom they are sent. Where would my poor perishing son have been if I had not asked you to pray for him, and help me to carry the burden of my soul? I had followed him round the world with my prayers. He came home unconverted, I brought his case right here. I cried: 'Men of Israel, help!' That son is converted, and I am sure it was in answer to prayer. Do not be wearied with the coming of these requests. Oh no! no! Let them come! Let us pray, not only here, but everywhere, for all for whom we are asked to pray; believing and hoping that God will answer our prayers." The tide of feeling was turned in regard to them, and they were always welcome. It came to be felt and acknowledged that they aided the life of the meeting. They came from all parts of the country, and from all sorts of persons—high and low—rich and poor—from bond and free. When answers to prayers began to be announced, fear flew away. Probably 100,000 requests for prayer have been before the meeting since the beginning; and notices of answers to prayers come nearly every day. No man can tell how many these have been. But they have been enough to fill heaven with exceeding joy.

Since the beginning there have been held about 4,000 meetings. They may be said to have been always fully attended from the first month till now. Thousands on thousands have come from all parts of the world, and had their spiritual strength renewed, and their faith increased. Hundreds have been converted in the meeting of whom we knew nothing till they revealed it in other places; and often thousands of miles away. A young man came into this meeting out of mere curiosity. He had heard and read of the meeting, and he came to see what it was. He was smitten of the Spirit at once, and in a short time converted, and told the meeting "how changed was his condition." He was a young merchant, and was in New York buying goods. He lived in a flourishing town on the banks of a great Western river far off; with not a single professor of religion in the town. As he stood before the meeting, he said: "The Lord has done great things for me, whereof my heart rejoices: and I go back to my home to raise the standard of the cross, and make confession every day, and everywhere, of my faith in Jesus. I shall try to establish a Sabbath School at once, and a prayer meeting, and I shall ask God to give me those who will help me in them."

He went, and was as good as his word. The Sabbath School and the prayer meeting sprang into existence at once. The Lord gave His Spirit. THREE large churches have been gathered. The town has become noted for its morality and religion; and our young friend stands at the head of a power in the Western country. How mysterious are the ways of God's grace. So God scatters His blessings. Hundreds have been the cases not very unlike the one just mentioned.

CHAPTER III.

FULTON STREET.

FULTON STREET is not a fashionable portion of the city, either for residence or business. It is a short street, running from the East River to the Hudson or North River. It is one of the busiest in the lower wards of this metropolis. On this street was situated the North (Dutch) Reformed Church, more than a century old, and, when built, considered almost out of the city. Here, in generations past, have worshipped men of mighty faith and prayer. But prayer and faith have grown in boldness, scope, and power beyond all that they saw, or dared to ask or think.

THE FULTON STREET MEETING.

Heard of with joy, with wonder, and almost with veneration all over the world! Designating a little daily shifting group of ordinary men and women, in a small commonplace apartment, saying and doing commonplace things in a very imperfect manner, very clearly the place is nothing, the name is nothing, the men are nothing. CHRIST IS ALL. Next to the wonder of his work is the wonder of his working *here*. The meeting is not local. It is œcumenical. People from all lands meet here almost daily. Christians from the remotest parts of the earth are of all men the most sure to find their way here, if brought to this metropolis.

Moreover, the meeting is not mainly in the body. Besides the Divine Spirit, who often fills the place, witnessing by works responsive to prayers, there are scores and hundreds of praying souls here daily from all parts of the world, who are here only in spirit. The place has become a centre both for suffering and sympathizing hearts throughout the Church universal. The daily business of the meeting is to pray for and with the churches everywhere which are pleading for fresh effusions of the Holy Spirit—the anxious parents, relatives and friends who wrestle for the conversion of those dearest to them, or for whom the Spirit and Providence of God have given them a charge over awakened souls who, in distant and dark places, are groping for a Saviour.

Such is the representative character of this meeting. Confined neither to place nor persons, it belongs to no one in particular—represents nobody: one church supplies the needed place; one man has the honor of being its doorkeeper, raising its songs of praise, takes the care of the room, sees that it is open at the proper time, and that a leader is at hand, and that the requests for prayer are placed before him. That is the beginning and end of the organization, or visible body of the thing.

But what shall we say of its INVISIBLE POWER? Its novelty is worn away in the eyes of the curious, but it is no less a *miracle* than ever. Nay, we are confident that its future is to be far greater than its past. As it belongs to no one, its present name and place may be forgotten. But the daily Union Prayer Meeting cannot stop. It must go on and increase. As was said of the everchanging river, while its elements come and go—the form remaining—the substance never dies.

The rapidity of the movement was as remarkable as anything else. The daily secular press took it up;—when did it ever do so before?—lending its power to promote a remarkable revival of religion not in the City of New York only, but in other cities, and in the country they took up the wonderful events which transpired in prayer meetings from day to day. They sent their reporters to the meetings to take notes of the incidents of the day, and the next morning by the breakfast-tables the accounts of the meetings were read by thousands of families in city and country. The news travelled as on the wings of the wind, and was eagerly devoured everywhere. To show how rapid and how great the influence it had in spreading the revival, we give illustrations such as follows:

A man, rising in the meeting, said: "I am a clergyman from Illinois. Just before I left home for New York, I was riding across the prairie on horseback, and saw some one running almost at right angles to my line of travel as if to head me off. So I held in my horse till he came up. When he came to my side he said he knew me, though I probably did not know him. I acknowledged I did not. He seemed to be a young man from eighteen to twenty years old, with a bright, ruddy, intelligent face.

"'Have you heard,' said he, 'of the great revival in New York?'

"I told him, 'I have heard of it.'

"'So have I,' he answered, 'and it has interested me greatly—I cannot tell you how much. I felt anxious to have a share in it.'

"I said, 'I am rejoiced to hear it.'

"He said, 'Do you see that bluff over yonder?'

"'I do.'

"'Well, just under that bluff there is a hollow place where I go for prayer, and this morning I have been there to pray—and now I think I can pray.'

"'How is that?' said I.

"'Oh! when I first began to go there I did not know how to pray—but I read how God answers prayer in Fulton Street and converts sinners, and I said why not here as well as there? So I began to pray under the bluff, and yesterday I think my prayer was heard and answered, and my sins have been forgiven, and you cannot imagine how happy I am. I thought when I saw you coming I must run and tell you how precious Jesus is to me.'

"So the dear youth talked on—his heart overflowing with love and gratitude to God for what He had done for him."

Another said: "You often hear that the reports of this meeting are doing good in the country. So they are, as I know from facts coming within my own knowledge. I assure you that many a sinner, hundreds of miles away, is awakened and brought to Christ by reading of the doings of this place of prayer. It is interesting to know how wide this influence is that saves souls from eternal death."

Another said: "I have been travelling for some time in eight States of the West. Coming out of Church one day, I was spoken to by a young man who inquired—'Do you belong to New York?'

"'I do.'

"'Do you ever go to the Fulton Street Prayer Meeting when at home?'

"'Yes, I go there often.'

"'Will you, when you next go, ask the meeting to pray for me?'

"'Most assuredly I will. But why do you wish to be prayed for?'

"'Oh because I am so miserable!'

"'How long have you been so miserable?'

"'For some time. I was first awakened by reading of *that* meeting, and how many sinners are turning to the Lord.'

"'Do you feel that you are a sinner?'

"'I am nothing else, as I well know. I want to know how a great sinner can be saved. Oh, it is dreadful to be as I am—a guilty wretch, and knowing no way of escape.'

"'Will you come to my room in the hotel for a little conversation and prayer at an hour I will name?'

"'Gladly I will come.'

"Prompt at the moment the young man was at my door knocking for admittance.

"As soon as he was in the room, he said: 'I can get no rest. I can neither eat nor sleep. I slept not a wink the last night. What shall I do?'

"'Believe on the Lord Jesus Christ.'

"'I knew you would say that. I have heard *that* before.'

"'Well you must hear *that* again, and if you will not believe on him, you are lost forever.'

"'What does Jesus say that I must believe?'

"'Jesus says—Him that cometh unto me, I will in no wise cast out.'

"'Can I come on that promise?'

"'Yes! believe him that he means just what he says.'

"'Oh! my heart is so stubborn I shall never believe unless he helps me.'

"'But he will help you. Why do you wish me to go to the Fulton Street Prayer Meeting and ask them to pray for you?'

"'Because God answers their prayers.'

"'True—and He is just as ready to answer yours.'

"'What shall I do then?'—great anxiety being depicted in his face.

"'Will you join me in prayer when I pray, kneeling right down here, and give yourself away to Jesus in an everlasting covenant to be his forever—do it here on your knees?'

"'I will try.'

"'No! no! trying is not doing it. Will you do it?'

"'*I will.*' He answered with great emphasis.

"I said, '*I* will pray—then *you.*'

"We fell on our knees.

"'Shall I tell Jesus you are on your knees to make a full surrender to him?'

"'YES! TELL HIM JUST THAT!'

"I felt that the time of the great decision had come, that the hour should decide the fate of a soul for the vast forever. I poured out a heart full of gratitude and joy for the salvation that was coming, or had already come, to this young man when he uttered those never-to-be-forgotten words,

'Tell Him just that.'

"When I ceased speaking, the young man, without the delay of a moment, broke out in such strains of thanksgiving as perfectly overwhelmed me. His heart was full of anthems of praise. His eternal life was begun."

CHAPTER IV.

INFLUENCE OF PRAYER ON THE COUNTRY.

THE church throughout the whole country was electrified by the reports of this wonderful spirit of prayer. Truly wonderful it was—for the presence and power of the Holy Spirit—for the number of conversions—for quickening power in the hearts of believers. It was great grace that had come down from above. There was no doubt about this. There was no cavilling, no opposition, no distrust. Regular reports of the meetings thrilled the hearts of Christians everywhere. Inquiries came pouring into the city in regard to this great work. Men came and saw and wondered. All believed it to be the amazing work of God. *We do not remember to have heard it spoken against* by any one in those days!

The work continued to increase and spread everywhere, distilling as the dew and as the small rain upon the dry and thirsty earth. Soon many a place became like a well-watered garden. The scenes of the winter of 1857 and 1858 in the religious world should be held in long remembrance.

The secular press in city and country soon entered into "The Great Revival," which was a standing head, under which were published reports from day to day—becoming an element of great religious power. It never can be known how much good was done by the secular press in spreading the news of what God was doing over the whole land by His Spirit in answer to prayer. Clergymen left their country homes for the time being, and came into the city to see for themselves. The city pastors did the same. Many went away with their hearts all aflame, and told their people of the "mighty works" of which they had been witness. The people heard them gladly. It was a theme—the Great Revival—always new, and always full of absorbing interest. Men of most piety and most talent were the first to appreciate the infinite importance of this work of grace, and they entered upon the appropriate duties of endeavoring to promote it with alacrity and great delight. The Fulton Street Prayer Meeting did much to repeat itself in the city and other cities without knowing it. This was done chiefly by prayer for the descent of the Holy Spirit upon the whole city, and other cities, and the country at large. Requests of this period were for the outpouring of the Holy Spirit upon this and other cities.

These requests have been preserved and are accessible to any one. We transcribe one, which is like many others of the same period:

"Will the Fulton Street Prayer Meeting, in their supplications, ask God to bestow upon our city and country the richest blessings of His grace in the largest measure, and enable us to open our mouths wide in the assurance that God will fill them. Pray that there may be a great turning to the Lord in this and in every place, and that converts may be multiplied as the drops of the morning. Let us pray, believing that God is able and willing to give the Spirit to all who ask Him all over the world."

The influence on other meetings for prayer was very soon very apparent in many ways, but chiefly in oneness of design and purpose, to pray for that one object—the baptism of the Holy Spirit. For this, daily prayer was offered in the Fulton Street Meeting. It was that the whole city might be swept as by a mighty rushing wind, and that the worst classes of society might be reached by Omnipotent grace and mercy. And prayer in this direction was answered in a most remarkable manner. Very soon meetings for prayer sprang up all over the city. Some of them were established in the habitations of iniquity—and they were admitted and felt to be heavenly places in Christ Jesus. The minutes spent in them flew on the wings of prayer. It was not in Fulton Street alone, but it was in many streets of this great city that the voice of prayer and praise was heard, and Christians of every name with one accord were bowed before the mercy seat. In all these, requests for prayer were presented, and answers to prayer were announced. None questioned—none dared to question—that this was the work of God. In all these meetings many testified to the gospel's saving power, men hardened in sin—desperate sinners—submitted themselves to the peaceful reign of Jesus. They spoke in joyful words of their own sweet experience, and of the happy hours they had spent with Jesus. They believed and trusted fully in him. No name was so precious as his. The hour and the act of consecration had come, and they had given themselves to the Lord in an everlasting covenant never to be forgotten. They spoke of Christ and him crucified wherever they went, and were not ashamed of the gospel of Christ. They witnessed a good confession before many witnesses. Many a rough, ungodly man acknowledged that he owed his salvation to the prayers of a praying mother —long since gone to glory. Some of these have gone to join the triumphant throng in heaven. Some remain to this day. It is very recently we heard one of these speaking in the Fulton Street Meeting. Something had been said about pious, praying mothers.

Said he: "I had such a mother whom I lost when I was nine years old. Oh! how I mourned for her. Cast all alone upon my own resources in this great and wicked city, I soon forgot my mother, and plunged into all manner of sin, in which I lived until I was thirty years old, and then God remembered his covenant, and I was summoned by the Spirit to come to my mother's Saviour and mine, for the pardon of all my sins on true repentance and faith in him. I was shocked and astonished at the time and circumstances of the call. I was arrested as suddenly as was Saul of Tarsus. I knew whom it was from. I knew my mother's prayers were unfolded in it. I did not hesitate to obey the call. I said my dear mother expected this—*she shall not be disappointed*,—that some day I would go to Jesus and cast myself on him.

"It was done years ago, when this meeting first commenced. Years ago! Oh! what happy years, *happy years!* I bear my testimony everywhere to the faithfulness of God in hearing and answering prayer. Oh! mothers!—mothers!"—he spoke in the utmost tenderness—"never give up your sons, be they ever so wayward, but pray and believe that they will be saved."

We looked around to see the speaker, and there stood a fine-looking man, of splendid proportions—every inch a man, bearing his testimony to the faithfulness of God in keeping his covenant with his mother.

This meeting soon began to be claimed as belonging to every other place, as witness the following:

A foreigner arose and said: "I call this a world's prayer meeting. I am a young man just over from Scotland, the land of Chalmers and Wardlaw, and great men whom you know." To show that this is a world's prayer meeting he read a most touching request from his young wife, that he would attend the Fulton Street Prayer Meeting as often as he could, while he was in the city, and then he would be safe amid the temptation. This young wife speaks of this meeting as if she had a personal interest and property right in it, and its influence is wide as the world, and precious as heaven.

"I cannot tell you how many hearts, far out over the sea, cluster around this meeting. I cannot tell you what hopes centre here, because this is a place of prayer, where the Lord overshadows you by his presence continually. We know that, with all things else, wickedness concentrates here—coming from Scotland, Ireland, England, Germany, from every place on the face of the earth. All know how New York is exposed to the coming in of iniquity like a flood; and, knowing all this, you will imagine that we look with great interest to this daily prayer meeting, as a bulwark against the flood."

CHAPTER V.

INFLUENCE UPON THE WORLD.

SELDOM has so profound an impression been made upon the religious communities as was wrought by the news of the Great Revival of 1858 which began in a little upper room in Fulton Street. The accounts published here were republished in all parts of the world, and were translated into almost all the spoken living languages. Soon the news came back to us that the revival was spreading into different countries of Europe, Asia, and Africa. The islands of the sea were awakened by the same invisible and amazing power, which attended here the wonderful movements of the Spirit. Ships came in from sea, in which some or all of the men of the crew and passengers had been converted, apparently without the intervention of any of the ordinary means of grace. Prayer meetings had been established on shipboard without any knowledge of the mighty displays of God's grace on shore. A ship-captain came into the Fulton Street Prayer Meeting and announced himself and all his crew converted on the voyage home. The Captain arose in the meeting, and addressing the leader, said: "We are all here Mr. Chairman, we are all here, and in answer to somebody's prayer—our fathers and mothers and brothers and sisters perhaps, and praying wives may have interceded for some of us and prevailed with a prayer-answering God. I am sure I stand here, a monument of amazing mercy, in answer to the prayers of my wife, who was converted after I left port, and I knew nothing about it. But from the moment of her awaking to a new life, and the prospect of a glorious immortality, she began to pray for my conversion, she begged for my soul to be given to the Lord Jesus before I should cast anchor in this port. And when I was converted, I said, 'Now all my men for Jesus Christ.' I soon had a regular daily praying service, without knowing anything about this meeting, and in a little time you could have heard the voice of prayer and praise all over the ship, and we have come up, a rejoicing company, to tell you what the Lord has done for us. I expected to find something new on arrival here. I often told the men we were among the days of prayer, and we should find our Christian friends praying for us. But on landing yesterday I was astonished to learn what God had been doing, and how many of our friends have been converted. When we were converted on the ship, we cried mightily unto the Lord that our friends might find the same grace which we have found."

From far-distant India and from California came requests for prayer just as naturally as they come from the region round about.

"To the Fulton Street Prayer Meeting:

"*Beloved in the Lord*—I have just received a letter from my brother (Rev. Dr. Scudder) in India, which contains the following words:

"'We hear good news from Tinnevally (a district of Southern India). The Lord is pouring out his Spirit there, and many are being converted. Persons have been struck down, as in the Irish revivals. In Arulupiens district also, God is displaying his wondrous and saving power. Oh! that he would visit us also, and cheer our hearts by turning multitudes unto himself. Stir up the churches at home to pray for this blessing.' Dear brethren! This appeal needs no comment from me. India stretches forth her hands towards you. The pleading voices of her perishing millions cry to you—'Pray for us, or we die.' Let me ask your special prayers for the Arcot mission. May God grant you faith, earnestness, importunity, and perseverance! Yours in the bonds of Christ,

JARED W. SCUDDER."

A gentleman stood with papers in his hand, and

said: "Perhaps no news ever surpassed in interest the news which we have from Ireland. And I question whether there ever has been, since the days of the Apostles, a more wonderful display of Divine power and grace, than has been manifested, and is now being manifested, in the county of Antrim, Ireland.

"Some months ago, there came over here a delegation from Ireland, to investigate the facts in regard to the great American Revival. They spent some months in this country and in Canada. They were able men, and the impression made upon them was deep and profound.

"They returned to Ireland, and they published a book, setting forth the amazing facts which they had witnessed, and of which they had gained information. They were Presbyterians, and they came as the representatives of five hundred Presbyterian Churches. Their book had a wide circulation. It was scattered broadcast over the land. It roused the spirit of religious inquiry and the spirit of prayer. And now you see what deep designs the Lord had in all this. The American Revival was to repeat itself in Ireland—that is, by its instrumentality, through these published accounts, the Lord intended to revive religion in Ireland, just as he had done in this country. And now we are permitted to see the glorious results. Why, these papers which I hold in my hand, are enough to electrify the coldest heart! Some of the mills and factories have had to suspend work, and some are running on half time—so great is the anxiety of the people to get to the places of preaching or prayer. They could not be restrained from going. They would go. Sometimes, if a clergyman was passing a mill, he would be called upon to stop and preach; and all the hands of the mill, to the number of several hundred, would pour out into the street to hear him. He mentioned some examples, to show how earnest this spirit was. A funeral procession was passing along the street, and a girl ran out of a mill, and asked if there was a clergyman in the rocession.

"'Yes,' was answered, 'there are two.'

"'Well, then, will not one please leave, and come and preach the gospel to us in the mill?'"

"One did leave; and there being no room in the mill, they assembled in the street to hear the sermon; and before it closed, many were crying aloud to God for mercy, and some were hopefully converted on the spot."

Another example was mentioned: "A minister came from the neighborhood to inquire in regard to these things, in one of these towns. He was asking a minister of the place, as they were walking along the streets:

"'Have you your Bible and Hymn-book with you?'" said the resident minister to the other.

"'Yes,' he answered.

"'Well, then, suppose you preach a sermon just here.'

"'But I have no congregation to preach to.'

"'Begin with singing the hymn, and we shall see if there will not be an audience.'

"They began to sing, and had not got through two

stanzas of the singing before the people came running together from every side to hear the sound of the gospel. When the hymn was concluded, and the prayer, the Lord touched the heart of the strange preacher, and the Spirit of God assisted him to lift up his voice in the ears of the multitude, and sinners on the spot were enabled to rejoice in Christ Jesus, with joy unspeakable and full of glory. They repented, and embraced him as a saviour, able, willing, ready, and mighty to save. This is only a faint illustration of the state of things in Ireland. All through the North of Ireland are the same gracious and glorious displays of Divine mercy in the salvation of souls."

"The following words were spoken by Rev. Dr. Murray, of Elizabeth, N. J.

"One year ago we had with us, in the anniversary of this meeting, a delegation from Ireland. It has been my privilege, since that time, to visit Ireland, and be a witness of the wonderful work of grace in that land. I was present at that great prayer meeting of 30,000 to 40,000. And such prayer! It was not for Ireland alone. I heard the most fervent, earnest prayer for America. I heard prayer for other countries. And how has God answered those prayers? The Church in Ireland has been doubled in two years. In some districts there is not a single family in which there is not family prayer, and in some congregations almost every person is converted. I visited a slate quarry in Wales, where 1,250 men were employed.

Bench above bench, they were at their work. Upon one plateau there were 70 or 80 huts, and you had to stoop to enter them. The men were assembled in these huts for dinner at 12 o'clock. They were allowed half an hour. When their simple meal was finished then every hut had a prayer meeting, so that there were 70 or 80 prayer meetings. Now what had been the effects upon these 1,250 men? Why, before the revival, a christian man could not live among them. It was as much as his life was worth. Now nearly all of those 1,250 men are praying men.

"We are not up to the times. I have felt it; I feel it now. What we need is the Holy Spirit to kindle more faith. We should pray for it, wait for it, and wait and pray. We should march on in our faith to the glorious promises and prophecies which are given us. You may have a cannon, and it may be a good one, and well loaded with powder and ball, and fitted to do eminent and signal execution. But you must have one thing more. You must have the spark of living fire. The Spirit is the living, spiritual fire which we must have. I have gone nowhere in all my travels that I have not heard of the Fulton Street Prayer Meeting. The influence has gone abroad over the whole world. The millenium is coming, but it is coming by prayer."

A clergyman arose in the meeting, and spoke with a foreign accent. He said he had never been in the meeting before, though he had heard and read much of the Fulton Street meeting. He had listened attentively to what had been said; and to the requests for prayers, and to the prayers themselves, which had been offered. And now he wanted to ask prayers, not for an individual, or a number of individuals, but for a people. The great armies were now encamped within sixty miles of the people for whom we should pray. He meant those pious Piedmontese, who were the descendants of the Waldenses. He said he had been a fellow student with twelve of the pastors who are now settled in the valleys and fastnesses of Piedmont, under the teachings of the illustrious D'Aubigne. In that country it was a felony to give away a tract or a Bible, a few years ago. He hoped we would pray for the people, who have stood firm to their covenant, and had borne their testimony, though it might cost them their liberty or their life. He hoped we would pray for the freedom of these people, and that God would so overrule the contests of nations, that the bondage of these people should cease.

Rev. Dr. John Thompson said that some of the noblemen of England and Scotland had come to this country, and on landing, had inquired for our great celebrities, and for this meeting as one of them. He said he knew of one nobleman, who had been several times in this meeting, though unknown to every person here. He went to Philadelphia, and under the guidance of our friend, George H. Stuart, Esq., he went into the prayer meeting, and in that meeting he told what the Lord had done for him in his conversion. We have with us, continued the speaker, a distinguished merchant to day from Glasgow—the New York of Scotland—with three ladies, his nieces, who came over here in their own yacht, and he hoped we might hear from him.

The gentleman arose, and with great modesty said he was not accustomed to speak in an assembly like this. He landed yesterday, he proceeded to say, and the first inquiry he made, as he stepped on shore was —"Where is Fulton Street?" He had heard of this meeting across the sea. In Glasgow, in Aberdeen, in Edinburgh, we have meetings for prayer, and they have been much blessed. There is much awakened religious interest among all classes, and in our churches of all names: Free Church—Established Church—and all denominations.

A gentleman arose and said he was just from London. He had never been in these meetings before. It was interesting, he said, to stand in the streets of London on every Sabbath day, and see the thousands who would gather into the streets around St. Paul's, and St. James' Hall, and Westminister Abbey, by four o'clock in the afternoon, and stand there till half-past 7 P. M., so that they might, if possible, get into these great places of convocation. Yet, Sabbath after Sabbath, this is so. Yet, to him, it was more interesting to stand here, upon this spot, consecrated to prayer, and the birthplace of much of the spiritual influence which has spread over the world and is spreading still.

On his passage homeward they encountered a terrible storm. The shaft of the steamship was broken, one wheel was disabled, and they expected, every moment, to go down. On board they had in one cabin several Catholic priests, and as many nuns or sisters of charity. They had also a very pious Methodist man. In the midst of the storm the priests were about to administer extreme unction, the last rite of the Church, by which all sin is supposed to be washed away. This Methodist had been with them, and to him one of the priests said: "I feel it my duty to tell you that we are about to administer extreme unction for the cleansing away of all sin. I must tell you that you are out of the true Church, and that if you die as you are you will be lost forever—you will be damned. Will you allow me to administer to you extreme unction, and thus save your soul?"

"Sir," said the Methodist, "I have been down to my state room for some time alone, with the High Priest of my profession. I have made a full and unreserved confession of all my sins. He has pronounced absolution from all my guilt. He has administered to me extreme unction. He has assured me that he is ready to receive me. He is mighty to save, and he tells me he can save, to the uttermost, all who come unto God through him. He has prepared me for death. I know that my Redeemer liveth. I am ready to have this vessel go down. I ask you if you really believe I need any preparation at your hands?" The priest was confounded, and said no more.

CHAPTER VI.

REMARKABLE CONVERSIONS.

In no prayer meeting in the world probably has Christ been more highly exalted than in the Fulton Street Prayer Meeting. Jesus and him crucified is the beginning, middle, and end of this meeting. He is the all in all to many, and the more he is exalted, the more tender and powerful does the meeting become. Said a clergyman of distinction:

"No man can describe or define this power of the Spirit. All we can know of it is by the effects which it produces. It is now just as it was in the days of our Saviour. 'The wind bloweth where it listeth, and thou hearest the sound thereof, but canst not tell whence it cometh, nor whither it goeth.' So is every one who is born of the Spirit. I have been in many revivals of religion, and I have seen many phases of the operations of the Holy Spirit; and there is nothing more difficult than to know how to instruct and to aid the sinner to find the Saviour when under this influence. Some make great mistakes at such times.

They talk too much, do too much, and thus do nothing, and worse than nothing. I have known a poor sinner's convictions all talked away, and the poor man goes away relieved, but, alas! not converted. He mistakes this relief for a change of heart, but after a time he finds that he is still 'in the gall of bitterness and bonds of iniquity.' That man is very apt to feel that he has tried religion and found there is nothing in it. You must yourself be under the power of the Spirit to know how to guide those that are. But be sure not to say too much. Be sure to put no dependence on what you say to lead that inquiring soul to Jesus. I have seen hale, strong men under this power of the Spirit, perfectly unmanned. I felt that I was standing on holy ground when standing in such presence. I dared say but a little. I felt that I must stand still and see the salvation of God. Now let me give some illustrations of this POWER OF THE SPIRIT. I will draw them from facts which have taken place within my own knowledge, and in connection with this meeting.

"Some time ago a man came into this meeting, in bodily health hale, hearty, and strong; in mind easy, joyous, happy—caring for nothing. He sat down in the meeting to enjoy, in his way, the exercises in mere idle curiosity. While sitting here he was struck under the most pungent conviction of sin. He was in great distress before the close of the meeting, and when it broke up he could not leave. He wept like a child. Though a hale, strong man, he was weak. His great strength departed from him. He was a wonder to himself, and to others. He was taken into a little room and prayed with. Little was said to him, a few encouraging passages of Christ's own words and promises were read to him, and gradually his mind was calmed, and the veil of his heart was lifted, and he laid hold on Jesus by a living faith, and his joy became unspeakable. It was full of glory. He took a decided and noble stand for Christ, and has ever since witnessed a good confession.

A FLEEING UNIVERSALIST.

"I will take another example from my own experience in a village some distance away, where I was then residing. It was a season of the outpouring of the Holy Spirit. We held morning prayer meetings every day, to spend before breakfast one half hour in earnest supplication for the conversion of sinners. We held night services every day of an hour long, the time being spent mostly in prayer.

"I looked out of my window one morning, while it was yet dusk, and saw a lady standing at my gate, leaning her head against a post, and evidently weeping bitterly. I knew her. She was a member of the church, and was an earnest consistent Christian. She was married to one of the most bitter Universalists I ever knew. I stepped down the steps to her, and asked, 'What is the matter?' She replied, 'Oh, my poor husband!—my dear husband! I had so hoped and prayed that he might be converted in this revival! And now he has rode away, and says he will not come back till this 'religious flurry' is over. What shall I do to bear up under this?'

"I said, 'It is near the time for prayer. We will go and lay his case before the Lord, and make *special request* that God will bring him back again under the power of the Spirit. The Lord can bring him home, and I believe he will do it. We must pray for him.'

"She dried her tears in a moment, and seemed to seize hold of this 'strong hope' as we walked to the place of prayer. We found the room crowded. It fell to my lot to lead the meeting. At the opening I stated the case of this Universalist husband who had undertaken to run away from the influences of the Spirit by fleeing into the country. I said we must all pray that the Holy Spirit may follow and bring him back again, show him his sins, and lead him to Jesus.

"The meeting took up the case with great earnestness, and I could not but feel that prayer would in some way be answered. But can you imagine our surprise when, at our evening prayer meeting, this same Universalist came in. After standing a few minutes, till the opportunity offered, he said:

"'I went away on horseback this morning, and told my wife I was going into the country to stay till this flurry is over. I rode right over the hills, back from the river, into the country, till I had got eighteen miles away. There on the top of a hill I was stopped as Paul was, and just as suddenly, and made to feel what a horrible sinner I am. I am one of the worst sinners that ever lived. I have lost my Universalism, and I know I must be born again, or I can never see the kingdom of heaven. Oh, pray for me that I may be converted. Nothing else will do for me.' He took his seat amid the tears and sobs of the whole assembly. You need not to be assured that the hour was full of prayer for this man's conversion.

"This strong and intelligent man, once one of the bitterest Universalists I ever knew, is now an elder of a Presbyterian church, and one of the most joyous, happy, energetic men of God you will meet in many a day; and great is the company of unbelievers whom he has led to Christ. He believes he was 'converted on the spot' in that prayer meeting."

Another example is the case of one who by some kind providence came to this meeting, in which he became interested to degrees unaccountable to himself.

THE YOUNG HUSBAND.

The case is that of a young man, intelligent, worthy as a moralist, fashionable, occupying a high social position, married to a gay, fashionable wife, living in one of the fashionable avenues in this city, himself, wife, and one sister making up the family, dwelling together in peace and comfort so far as this world is concerned, and entirely given up to its pleasures.

In the progress of events that young man was brought under the amazing and mysterious power of the Holy Spirit—he never could tell how. For many days he was sad and sorrowful, and his wife and sister knew not what to make of the fact that one so full of fun and frolic and gayety and nonsense, as well as sense, should all at once become taciturn and indifferent to all the pleasure of the world within his reach. Was he sick? or had he met with some great reverse in business? or what was the matter? They could not tell.

The young man all this time was coming daily to these meetings, and his family knew it not. At length he found joy and peace in believing in Jesus. Going home, he said to himself, "Now I must serve the Lord Jesus, and I will begin at once. I must go home, and tell what the Lord has done for my soul, read the Bible, and pray with my family." The tempter said:

"Not to-night; not so soon." "Yes," said the young man, "*to-night.*" "No! no!" said the tempter; "don't be in such a hurry. Wait till you get a little stronger; wait a few days."

"I cannot wait a few days; I must begin at once. I will pray in my family to-night."

"Yes," said the tempter, "and you will fail to-night, and break down, and make a fool of yourself."

"Oh! I have made a fool of myself all my life, and to-night I must begin to act a sensible part, and do my duty. I must pray," said the young man.

"You must pray, must you?" the tempter rejoined. "What do you know about prayer? You have never prayed, you have never learned the alphabet of prayer scarcely, and you had not better begin to do to-night what you have never done in all your life—pray before your wife and sister. You don't know the language of prayer. You will surely fail and make yourself ridiculous; and then think how much harm you will do."

"I must do my duty," the new convert rejoined. "I am not responsible for consequences."

"Yes, you are responsible for consequences," said the tempter. "Wait a few days. Get a little experience. Do you not know how important that is? Experience clinches the nail. The meeting is all the time talking about experience, and you have no experience worth speaking of. Besides, you don't know that you are a Christian. This is all a sudden business with you. Wait till you know what this all is."

"I shall not wait. I shall pray to-night. Get thee behind me, Satan. I must pray, and I will pray. I have told Jesus all about it, and I am sure that He will help me."

When he went into his house the young man sought his library, and there he poured out his heart to God. He confessed the struggle which he had, and he prayed for grace to do his duty, and make open confession of his faith in his divine and adorable Saviour, and asked for grace to own and honor Him.

He went into his sumptuously furnished parlor. The gas was shedding its mellow light from the burners. His wife and sister were there. The time for prayers had come. The wife noticed with a kind of awe the great change in her husband's countenance, but said nothing. This wife he loved as he did his own soul. He turned, and said in a tender, loving voice, which she felt:

"My dear, have you any objection to our having family worship?"

"Not in the least," she answered with true politeness, "if it is your pleasure." At the same time she regarded him with perfect amazement, and wondered what would come next. She could not have been more astonished than she was.

"Then get the Bible if you please," said the husband, "and draw up around the table, and we will read and pray."

He read, and then he kneeled down to pray; but he observed that he alone was kneeling as he opened his mouth to speak in prayer. Both wife and sister were sitting bolt upright in their seats. This disconcerted and embarrassed him for a moment; and sure enough the tempter's prophecy had come true.

At length he burst forth into the imploring cry, "God be merciful to me a sinner;" and God was merciful. His tongue was loosed now, and he poured forth an earnest prayer that God would have mercy on his dear wife and sister, and convert them on the spot.

As he went on the heart of his wife was overcome. She slipped down from her seat, knelt beside her husband, put her arms around his neck, and ere she was aware her prayer was, "God be merciful to me a sinner," and she burst into a flood of weeping and sobbed aloud.

The sister knelt down on the other side of him, and put her arms around him. She sought a Saviour's mighty power to save.

The peace of that family now flows as a river, and their salvation as an overflowing stream, and all are hoping with assurance forever that their sins are forgiven, and their iniquities are blotted out to be remembered no more.

A TOUCHING INCIDENT.

A young man from Chicago had been speaking and telling the story of his conversion, and asking the prayers of the meeting on the labors in which he is engaged. The account of his conversion was very tender and touching, and produced a thrill of deep emotion in the audience. He said he belonged to a band of young men who make it their business on the Sabbath afternoons to go two, three, or four together, and hold religious services where the people are cursed with grog-shops all around.

They go right into the drinking saloons, and get

leave if they can to sing and speak and pray for a few minutes, and generally they will be accorded permission, and they endeavor to make their words few and earnest. By this means they win some souls to Jesus.

When the young man had concluded, an old merchant arose and said the experience of the young man which has been just now related had very much affected him. Said the merchant:

"Four years ago, that young man was in my employ— a wild, thoughtless young man, full of life, and devoting that life to the service of the devil. Now he is preaching Christ in the very sinks of iniquity in which he used to be engaged.

"I am reminded how the grace of God overtook me. I was never given up to many of the vices in which many engage. There was an exception of horse-trotting, which I was passionately fond of. I had won nine hundred dollars one morning, and was returning home. I was struck with a sense of sin as suddenly as Saul of Tarsus was. I was shown my sins with such an intense illumination of the Holy Spirit of their enormity, that I cried out aloud in my wagon as I was riding along. I was called upon to enter my soul in a race for heaven. I found I had to put in my horse too. It was this way. The Spirit through my conscience said:

"'You must not trot this horse for money another time.'

"To this I consented. Again it said:

"'You must not sell to a man who will trot him.'

"I said, 'I am agreed to that too.'

"Horse and self never went near a race-course again. I kept my agreement, and accepted the terms, and entered my soul for a race to heaven. I am running in it now. When I covenanted with Jesus, it was to give up sin and take him for my all in all, and give myself wholly to him."

We know this New York merchant well. He is very often in the meeting, and is one of the most happy, joyful, consistent Christians whom we have ever known. His very countenance is full of cheer, and he does not fail to let his light shine.

AFTER THE MEETING.

The regular meeting had been dismissed, and it was found that one or two young men were unwilling to go until they found him whom their souls were seeking—the Lord Jesus Christ. There were some remaining, after the regular exercises had closed, standing around in groups here and there, telling how much they enjoyed the meeting.

A young man approached one of these groups of a Presbyterian minister, an elder of the same denomination, two Reformed (Dutch) clergymen, and two or three others. He wished to know if he could be saved then.

"Yes," he was answered.

"I want to be saved on this very spot—in this very hour—before we leave the room. Can this be?" he inquired.

"Yes," said one in the little company. He explained in a few simple sentences what it was to be saved, and how God applies the blessings of the atonement to the soul of the sinner. Said he:

"All you have to do is to let the Lord Jesus do it all, and commit your soul into his hands for time and eternity, and believe that he will do all that he has promised on your exercising faith and confidence in him beyond all doubt and question. You do not help him to save you, but you commit to him your soul in the fullest confidence that he is able and willing to do all he has promised. And what has he promised? He has promised that he will save to the uttermost all who come unto God through him. He has promised, 'Him that cometh unto me I will in no wise cast out.' You must believe, and receive these and all other promises of Jesus without a shadow of doubt or distrust, and give yourself to him beyond the possibility of a recall —to be no more your own, but Christ's—consecrating yourself body and soul to him, by whose blood all your sins are washed away, and you become united to him by a living faith in bonds which are to last forever. Are you ready to make this consecration now?"

"I am."

"Do you take all Christ's work as done for you, and on your trusting in him, believe in him as accepting you and saving you now—here on this spot—in this blessed room of prayer?"

The young man answered: "I take Christ's sufferings and death as endured for me; his blood as shed for me; his promises as made to me; and by these I am to die unto sin daily and live unto holiness, all through the grace which he gives. The only doubt I have is about the degree and strength of my faith."

"Ah! with the strength of your faith you have nothing to do; but with the *fact* of your faith you have all to do. If you confess your sins, God is faithful and just to forgive you your sins, and to cleanse you from all unrighteousness. Can you fully believe all that?"

"I can say, 'Lord, I believe; help thou mine unbelief,' answered the young man, with deep solemnity and emotion. It was a solemn moment; the hinges were turning on which the salvation of a soul was depending.

"Let us get down on our knees," said the man of God, "and pray." In a moment all were bending, and the voice of prayer was lifted up, first one praying, and then another, and then another, all short and to the matter in hand, with uncommon fervor. Last of all came the voice of the young man, in a clear, intelligent manner, with the deepest sincerity, telling Jesus that he believed all he had said, and he accepted all he had done, and he promised to do all he required for time and eternity.

"Lord, I am thine, forever thine,
Purchased and saved by blood divine."

Then came a voice of thanksgiving and praise for what God had done by his spirit in bringing this young man to the feet of Jesus, and leading his heart and mind in making this personal and everlasting consecration to his service. Said the prayer, "Jesus, keep this young man in thine eternal keeping, and save him with an everlasting salvation." This ended this after-service prayer-meeting, in the course of which all present believe that a poor lost sinner was saved and made alive forevermore. It was a miracle of grace.

Such occurrences are not unfrequent of sinners finding peace in believing, even before leaving the room, who when they entered it were borne down under a weight of despair.

THE SUPERINTENDENT'S STORY.

A gentleman arose who is the superintendent of a mission Sabbath school connected with a Reformed church in Brooklyn. He is remarkable for his earnestness, and success in his labors of love among the neglected and low classes of the city.

He said that in the first year of this meeting he brought the case of four boys here for prayer. They were youths from twelve to fourteen years of age. They were bright boys—the children of poor parents. They were attentive upon the Sabbath school, and made good progress in gaining a knowledge of divine truth. Now see how God answered our prayers in their behalf. They were all converted, and made a public profession of their faith in Christ. I have kept track of my four boys from the time of their conversion until now. They are all earnest Christians. One of them poured out his life-blood for his country in the late war. The three others studied for the ministry, and are all now settled as pastors of churches. I lately spent a Sabbath with one of them. I went up the North River to a little village where I found him in a nice parsonage, settled over a small but increasing congregation, worshipping in a beautiful church.

The two others are well settled over prosperous churches. Now all this and more is in answer to prayers offered in this meeting fourteen years ago. How true it is that God is faithful to his promise— "Ask and ye shall receive."

"DO WE PRAY BELIEVING?"

Said one, rising quickly to his feet, "Do we pray believing? I am here to give you an example of answer to prayer. I feel as if I had a duty to do it, to encourage you to pray believing."

The speaker was a man about fifty years old. He looked like an intelligent, hard working farmer, belonging to that class who are always up and doing what their hands find to do.

"I am from Saratoga County," he continued, "and I consider I owe it to this Fulton Street Prayer Meeting to give you the following facts:

"Some time ago a pious, devoted Christian mother having two sons, young married men, in good standing in society, and heads of young and rising families, became exceedingly anxious for their conversion. It was an agony of desire. I never saw greater mental distress than she was in. She seemed to be imbued with the spirit of prayer for her children's conversion, and would not be denied. She came to me with her soul thus heavily burdened. She wished me to write to this meeting and ask you to assist her by your prayers. I wrote a very earnest appeal, and sent it forward to be read in your hearing, and by you to be presented to the throne of grace in prayer.

"I kept track of that request. I knew the very day and hour it was presented here. These two sons lived twelve miles apart, and knew nothing of their mother's prayers and tears. They knew nothing of the request sent to this meeting, for that was done under my own hand, and no one but the mother and myself knew anything about it.

"Now mark what followed. These two men on the same day, at night, after they had been prayed for here, without concert with each other, established family prayer, and thus commenced a religious life. The family altar was erected, and thus their confession of faith in Jesus was made, and these two men, whom I well know, are now faithful and devoted Christians.

They both live in Saratoga County, and I see them often. They were converted as we believe, on the very day they were prayed for here. Some one—perhaps many—offered believing prayer. Faith is the great element of successful prayer, and it must have been yours and the mother's prayers which prevailed with God."

"IS THERE SALVATION FOR ME!"

"*Oh, yes! there is salvation for just such a sinner as you!*" An old missionary arose in the meeting and said this; and he continued:

"I was called to visit a man at 12 o'clock last night, who was in great distress of mind. It was at the solemn midnight hour that I entered the poor man's room. Everything betokened misery. I sat down by the bedside of the poor man, but I had nothing to say. I seemed to be shut up to silence. I wondered that I could say nothing, inasmuch as I had come for that purpose. I wondered at myself. It was a still meeting.

"At length the man burst forth with the exclamation, 'O! what a dreadful sinner I am! What a wretched, wicked man!' He turned his face from me as he said it. Still I had no words. I said to myself, 'What does this mean?' I was disappointed in myself.

"In a few minutes the man exclaimed, 'Can there be any salvation for me!' Then my mouth was opened, and I said, 'Oh, yes! there is salvation for just such a sinner as you!' And I began and preached to that poor, miserable man, Jesus. I told him of the full satisfaction which Jesus had made in offering himself up once for all, that whosoever believeth on him might not perish, but might have everlasting life. I told him that all he had to do was to believe the testimony which Christ gave of himself: that he came to seek and to save them that are lost; he came not to call the righteous, but sinners to repentance; that his promise is to save to the uttermost all who come to God through him. 'This is a faithful saying, and worthy of all acceptation, that Jesus Christ came into the world to save sinners.' And he has declared, 'Him that cometh unto me I will in no wise cast out.' Now he says to any and every sinner, 'Though your sins be as scarlet they shall be white as snow, and though they be red like crimson they shall be as wool. He that believeth on me, though he were dead, yet shall he live.' 'So there is salvation for just such a sinner as you.'

"So I continued to preach Jesus as willing and mighty to save. I had words enough, for my heart was full of thanksgiving that we have such a Saviour to set before a sinner ready to perish.

"Oh, how did that poor man lay hold of the truth, bow to the truth, accept with unutterable joy the truth as it is in Jesus. I told him there was no peradventure, no mistake about it. He might have salvation now and salvation forevermore. And I verily believe that poor sinner was saved in that self-same hour. I left him rejoicing, and he has been rejoicing ever since. I prayed with him and commited him to God, to be kept through faith unto salvation, ready to be revealed in the Great Day."

So God displays the riches of his grace in saving the chief of sinners.

A JUDGE ON THE FLOOR.

A judge of the Court of the Queen's Bench, from one of the British provinces, seized an opportunity to address the meeting. He said:

"You do not know how much these meetings are doing in building up the kingdom of Christ. The reports of this meeting go far and wide. They are translated into other languages and scattered among the nations of the earth. Many a Christian heart is cheered and roused to Christian action. Why, I could tell you many incidents which have come under my observation, of good done through the influence of this meeting. I will give you only one. It was one night I was called to attend a case of great distress. I found a man sunk down in deep despair by reason of intemperance. I found the poor inebriate a man of high education and culture, and his wife an educated and cultivated woman. I had read of the cases in this meeting, reformed and saved, in answer to prayer, for I read the reports of this meeting every week. I took the man and his wife home to my house. I treated him as I would a brother, and now that man is a member of the same church with myself, and is a useful and happy Christian, and adorns his Christian profession by a well-ordered life. He is one of my class.

"I know of cases where our churches have asked you to pray for the outpouring of the Holy Spirit, and the showers of divine grace have come down in answer to prayer. I have the means of knowing something of the wide extent of your usefulness from an extensive correspondence. May God continue to pour upon this meeting the spirit of grace and supplication, and bless you in the future as He has done in the past. For ten years I have read the reports of this meeting, and in common with thousands on thousands I have been cheered and encouraged by them."

A young man arose and said he must bear witness to the great cardinal truth that Jesus saves the vilest sinners. He said:

"I found that out in this meeting. I came to Jesus as I was. I claimed no merit in coming. I came as a poor, vile, undone wretch who could do nothing for himself; helpless as well as vile; totally ruined. I came to be saved. Oh, how I rejoice that the degree of ill desert has nothing to do with our Saviour's willingness to save. How I rejoice that all power is committed to his hands, and that whosoever sins he remits they are remitted. And as far as the East is from the West, so far he removes our transgressions from us. He has no reproaches for me. He does not leave me in disgrace. He does not remind me what a base sinner I have been—unlike men.

"When a man has wronged a fellow-man, or has done some disgraceful act, the disgrace sticks to him, though he has confessed and forsaken his sin a thousand times. A man says, 'I can forgive, but I can never forget.' Not so with Jesus. He blots out the handwriting which is against us, to be remembered no more forever."

One said he wished to state how God had dealt with a request which was laid before the meeting some time ago, not many days. In answer to prayer, a brother had been converted and a child restored to health, whose father—a physician—had said could not possibly survive. For these and other mercies bestowed in answer to prayer, he had come from his country home on purpose to ask the meeting to join him in thanksgiving. He led the meeting in this prayer of thanksgiving, which was very touching.

WHITEFIELD'S LITTLE SERMON.

A gentleman was in the meeting who said he once went to hear Mr. Spurgeon in London, and in the course of his sermon, to illustrate the power and importance of personal fidelity, he related the following of Rev. Mr. Whitefield: He carried his personal fidelity so far that he never let an opportunity pass without speaking to such as he might on the subject of religion. It was rumored and believed all over

England that he never stayed over a night in a family that he did not leave them all Christians when he departed the next morning.

A family of husband and wife and five children had become anxious about their salvation, and yet they walked in darkness and knew not what to do. The husband said to the wife one day, "Now you know I am not a Christian, though I want to be; and you are not a Christian, and yet you would be if you only knew how to be; and none of our five children are Christians. Now let us send for Mr. Whitefield to come and stay with us three days, for they say all become Christians where he stays; and let us entertain him in the best manner we can, and do all we can to make his stay with us comfortable." So they sent to him a very urgent invitation to come, and they would do all they could for his comfort while he tarried the three days. They were people well off in the world and were able to carry out what they undertook. So the good man came.

The first day passed and nothing was said on the subject of religion. The second day passed and ended in the same way, and the third, and the morning came and he was gone, and not one word had been dropped on the subject of salvation. All this time they had been so assiduous they had perfectly overwhelmed him with their attentions. They said one to another,

"What does this mean? What does it mean?" And they were in real distress. Finally the husband went up to Mr. Whitefield's room to look around and see if he had left any instruction or any message for them.

Mr. Whitefield, as he was about leaving, had taken his diamond ring, and on the pane of a window had written these words:

"*One Thing Thou Lackest.*"

As soon as the man had found it he called to his family down stairs, "Come right up here; here it is— Mr. Whitefield's little sermon; come right up here quickly; here it is," said the man, as they came trooping up with all haste. "Here it is," said the man; "true, every word true. I have lacked the one thing, and so have you my dear wife, and so do you my dear children. We all lack the one thing."

"I thought it strange," said the wife, "but the good man looked so sad. So SAD when he went away and bid us all good-bye. Now I know why he looked so sad. He knew we lacked the *one thing.*"

A poor girl writes to the meeting. She has written five or six times before, always in great distress of mind, and always describing herself as a very wicked girl. Now a letter comes full of rejoicing. She says, when she found the meeting did pray for her, her heart was so filled with joy and melted with sorrow, that she fell on her knees, and begged God to have mercy on her, and forgive all her sins, "and He did," so she says and believes, and her heart is so full of joy that she calls on the meeting to unite with her in her song of praise to Jesus, so plenteous in mercy, so ready to forgive.

Many a hard heart has been melted by hearing what the Lord has done for the soul of another, so that he has found out that he has a soul of his own to be saved or lost. Many an unbeliever has been subdued to the belief and love of the truth by means of the religious experience of some one who has lately come to the knowledge of the truth.

THE LEADER A CONVERT.

The leader of the meeting was lately converted. He was a fine looking young man, apparently about 30 years old, very intelligent, conducting the exercises with great modesty and propriety. He said:

"Perhaps some of us heard with horror those words of the rejection of Jesus when they said, 'Away with Him, away with Him.' Oh! I said, by my language and conduct for thirty years, those same words when Jesus was proposed to me as a Saviour—'Away with Him, away with Him.'"

The words he uttered in a hushed voice, as if almost overcome with his own emotions. There was a tenderness in his voice which touched every heart. Tears started in many eyes as he added:

"I am before you as one who hopes in the amazing mercy of this same Jesus, so often and so long rejected. I feel I was just as guilty as the Jews who first uttered these cruel words. It is but a short time since I first noticed his wounded hands and feet and side, and felt that He was wounded for my transgressions and bruised for my iniquities, and that the chastisement of my peace was upon Him, and by his stripes I am healed. It is but very lately that I was led to behold Him as Thomas did, and exclaim, as he did, 'My Lord and my God! Whom have I in heaven but Thee? and there is none upon earth that I desire besides Thee.' I bear my humble testimony to the willingness of Jesus to forgive sin. I have taken him to be my Saviour—

"'Mine entirely—through eternal ages mine.'

"If there is a poor, weary, heavy-laden sinner here, I exhort you to come to Jesus. Try Him. Try His love and mercy. Cast yourself upon Him, for He careth for you. Now let us sing the hymn—

> 'I lay my sins on Jesus,
> The spotless lamb of God;
> He bears them all and frees us
> From the accursed load.'"

When sung, one and another and another, recently converted young men, gave brief accounts of their hopeful conversion within a few days past. They had resolved to lift the banner high, and display their adhesion to Jesus.

CHAPTER VII.

COMING TO THE LIGHT.

An elderly Scotch clergyman arose in one of the meetings and said:

"Yesterday being the Sabbath, I witnessed an incident worthy of being mentioned here. A little girl five years old had been admitted into a Sabbath-school, and as she became acquainted with the truths of religion, she made these the matters of conversation with her mother, who was ignorant of all the great truths of the gospel. The 'little child' became exceedingly intelligent in these great doctrines which teach our lost condition by reason of sin, and our way of recovery and salvation through the Lord Jesus Christ.

"The mother became very anxious to know how she might be saved. And she had to go to her little girl to learn the way to Jesus. The little child had been taught of the Spirit, while the poor mother groped in darkness. The one walked in the light, while the path of the other was shrouded in gloom. She knew not at what she stumbled. She often had to go to the child to be taught what she did not know. The child got her instruction from the Sunday-school lesson out of the word of God.

"Yesterday I heard that mother and that little child tell their religious experience, make public profession of their faith in Christ, and receive the ordinance of baptism and admission into the church.

"When the mother came to tell how she floundered in her ignorance of the way of life to find it, and how she had to go to her little child to know what she should do in her perplexity, it was very touching, and drew tears from many eyes. 'And when I was striving to DO SOMETHING,' said the mother, 'to have my child come to me and say, That's not the way, mother,—don't you remember what the hymn says, mother:

> 'Come lay your deadly doing down,
> Down at Jesus' feet.'

All you have to do is to take to your soul what Jesus has done. Don't you remember the hymn says:

> 'Jesus paid it all,
> All the debt I owe;
> Nothing either great or small,
> Remains for me to do.'

All you've got to do is to believe that, mother. Can you believe that? So my Bible and my teacher tell me. Jesus has done it for me. Paid it all. He has taken the stumbling-blocks out of the way. The path is all smooth, so that we can run in it. Don't you see, mother?'

"At length the mother did see. She hugged the little preacher to her bosom, and submitted to be led by her little child. And when mother and daughter stood together hand in hand to take the vows of God upon them, there were no dry eyes in all that great assembly. And no wonder! Who *could* refrain? Who would? I would not, others could not. The hearts of the whole assembly melted within them. It was not so much at what we saw as at what we felt. It was the fulfilment of the glorious promise, ' And a little child shall lead them.' "

An old sailor, in his red woollen shirt, arose to pray, and pray he did with a trembling voice, the big tears rolling down his cheeks:

"We thank Thee, O Father, because thou hast hid these things from the wise and prudent, and hast revealed them unto babes, for so it seemed good in thy sight.

" O dear Lord Jesus, thou knowest how years and years, long years, I lived in sin and misery, ignorant of Thee, and rejecting the great salvation. I could see nothing in Thee that I should desire Thee. But now, when my eyes have been opened, what wonders of love and beauty do I behold, so that my heart longs for Thee with great desire, and my mouth is ready to exclaim, ' Whom have I in heaven but Thee, and there is none upon earth that I desire beside Thee. O Jesus, one sight of Thee is worth more to my soul than all other sights. Often when I have been looking, it has seemed that I could bear no more, and then the view has been more rapturous, and I have cried out, ' Oh! the depth of the wisdom and knowledge of God. How unsearchable are Thy judgments, and Thy ways past finding out.'

"I thank Thee that Thou canst reveal this love to babes, and make the children leaders of the parents to find their way to Jesus. Oh, I thank Thee for the riches of thy grace revealed to the most vile and sinful. Thy precious blood can cleanse me from all sin, though my sins have been as scarlet and crimson dyes. Lord Jesus, I receive thy kingdom as this 'little child,' with the utmost simplicity, and with unquestioning faith. I remember the horrible pit from whence I was taken. I praise Thee, O Jesus, that I was ever delivered out of it. And when no eye pitied this poor, undone wretch, Thine own eye pitied, and Thy own arm wrought my salvation. Oh! eternity will be too short to utter all Thy praise."

It was a wonderful prayer, for there was an unction about it that no language can describe. It seemed to be a pity to have the prayer end so soon. People forgot the man who was standing there in his red shirt, while they became absorbed in the great theme with which he closed his prayer.

THAT SAD FACE.

There are cases of great mental and spiritual distress in the Fulton Street Prayer Meeting. They are met with very often. The secrets of aching hearts are not all revealed, and we do not know them. But sometimes the countenance betrays the distress within. Who can tell the agony of a heart certain of its guilt, but uncertain of the way of securing justification and pardon.

"I am unspeakably miserable," says one in her request for prayer. "What shall I do?" Poor soul! she knows not where to lay her burden down. She has not yet found the Saviour's feet. She was in the meeting—coming in with a sister, both of them strangers, and both supposing that they would be unrecognized. They did not dream how much that sad face would reveal. It was easy to see who was in this great mental and spiritual trouble. She was a lady in middle life. She seemed to have come in from the country, and to be under the care of a pious and devoted sister who lives in the city. She sat through the meeting, but a little distance from the writer, where the working of her countenance could be observed. There sat on that face the picture of despair. It was the saddest of all sad faces. Who can tell what that suffering was which calls itself "unspeakably miserable?"

When the services were over we both met in the aisle, and it was evident that she wanted to speak. So I inquired:

"Have you enjoyed the meeting?"

"I can hardly say that," said she. "I cannot enjoy anything. But I have been glad to be here."

"Are you anxious to be a Christian?"

"Very anxious. It is an agony of anxiety."

"There is One who has said, 'Come unto me all ye that labor and are heavy laden, and I will give you rest.'"

"I know it—I know all about it, and could say the same to another. And yet practically I know nothing about it. I do not know what that one word means—that Come. I do not know how to come to Him."

"Do not know?—how can you say that?"

"I know intellectually, but I do not know practically. Do you know that the heart is blind?" She spoke with a voice of despair.

"Yes, I know it," I replied.

"Now if the heart does not understand, how am I to come? Is it not said, 'With the heart man believeth unto righteousness?' Now, if the heart will not believe, what can be done? Can you tell me?"

"No, madam! I cannot tell you. All I can do is to repeat the invitation of the Saviour, 'Come unto me.' That is all you have to do, and until that is done, nothing is done."

"Do you not remember that the same Saviour has said, 'No man can come unto me unless the Father who has sent me draw him?' How can I come until I am drawn?"

"Are you waiting till you are compelled to come? There is no coming in thus waiting. If you do thus you will never come."

"What shall I do?" She looked with a despairing look.

"Do?" said I, "do? Do as the poor prodigal did,

and say, 'I will arise and go to my Father.' Do just as he did. He did arise, and went to his father."

"How can I do it? The same difficulty remains. I know not what is the mental process, and if I did, and my heart says 'I will not,' what am I to do? How can I overcome that *will not?*"

"You must overcome it, or you will be numbered among those concerning whom Christ has said, 'Ye will not come to me that ye might have life.'"

"What shall I do then first?" She evidently made the inquiry in all sincerity. I answered:

"The first thing, and the second thing, and the third thing you have to do, and everything you have to do, is to believe on the Lord Jesus Christ, and you shall be saved."

"Can you tell me *how* to believe?"

"I cannot."

There was a pause. She stood in deep thought, then she said:

"If you cannot tell me, and no one can, how am I to know how to believe?"

"You can know how to believe by believing. There is no other way. It is a matter of the heart. It is an exercise of faith, and faith is the exercise of the heart. It is not a matter of reason, but of faith."

The lady stood in deep thought for a moment, then she said:

"This whole subject of personal religion seems to me involved in the deepest mystery. You say I ought to believe, and yet you say you cannot tell me how to believe. You tell me I am saved if I believe on the Lord Jesus Christ, and I am forever lost if I do not. Why should God tell me what to do to be saved, and not tell me how to do it?"

"I suppose," said I, "you may be the mother of children whom you dearly love?"

"Yes," she answered, her face brightening up, "I have children, and I love them dearly."

"Can you tell me how you love them?"

"I cannot tell *how* I love them. I was made to love them, and I should be an unnatural and cruel mother if I did not love them."

"Exactly so; and those children, I doubt not, love you?"

"Very much."

"Suppose they did not, and you should tell them they ought to love you, and they would if they could only be told *how*, could you tell them *how?*"

"I could not. I could only tell them it was their duty to love me, and they would be cruel if they did not. They were made to love me."

"Just so you are made to love God, and you ought to love Him without His telling you how you can do it. The *how* is no part of inquiry. You have no right to raise the question how you shall do what God requires you to do. You are to believe that God cannot command you to do what is unreasonable. I cannot tell you how to exercise any power or faculty of your mind. You—yourself—cannot tell how you exercise the powers and faculties of your mind. When you are commanded to believe on the Lord Jesus Christ, why should you not do it, because it is commanded, without the hesitation of a moment? When Christ says, 'Come unto me, all ye that labor, and are heavy laden, and I will give you rest,' why should you stand out to have the manner of your coming explained? All you have to do is to come, and your weary heart shall find rest. He condescends to assure you when He says, 'Him that cometh unto me I will in no wise cast out.' And again He says, 'Whosoever will, let him come and take of the water of life freely.' These are precious promises, and they mean you and me, and every sinner who will come. 'Believe on the Lord Jesus Christ and thou shalt be saved.' Glorious promise made to every sinner! 'The Spirit and the Bride say, Come. *Now* is the accepted time. *Now* is the day of salvation.'"

She stood weeping. I added:

"Now you are to believe all that God says in His Word simply because *He says it* with an unwavering faith."

"May I not reason about believing?"

"No, no." She looked surprised.

"No! Faith is above reason. Reason has no authority here. Reason is on a lower plane, and has no voice over faith. Faith is one of the attributes of the soul. To reason is to drive faith away. We believe on the simple word and promise of God. Reason must not step in to ask *why* nor *how*. Reason has not a word to say about it. The fact being settled that a promise has been made, it is a sin and shame to disbelieve. God is worthy of all our faith and love. 'Hath He said, and shall He not do it? Hath He spoken, and shall He not make it good?'"

All this dialogue was the work of a few minutes. The lady stood weeping and hesitating. She at length said:

"I think I see this matter in a new light. I must believe without asking how I can believe. Is that so?"

"It is just so. There is not a saint in heaven who can tell *how* he came to believe, and there is not a Christian on earth can tell anything about *how*. We cannot tell how the gulf between belief and unbelief is bridged over. We step from one spiritual condition to the other—we cannot tell how. The once spiritually blind cannot tell how he received spiritual sight. All he can say is, 'Whereas I was blind, now I see.' So of the gulf between belief and unbelief, we cannot tell how we got over. All we can say is Jesus helped us over."

"And will He help me over?" she inquired with eagerness.

"To be sure He will. He is the Way, the Truth, the Life, to every one who believes on Him. Can you not believe Him?"

She looked up in my eyes with a beaming face, and then heavenward she looked as she exclaimed, "Lord, I believe. Help thou my unbelief."

She was no longer unspeakably miserable, but she

rejoiced with a joy which was unutterable and full of glory. We saw her after the meeting the next day as she and her sister were passing out.

"Have you found Jesus?" said I.

"I hope I have found Him. He is unspeakably precious. I believe I have found Him in answer to prayer."

It was no longer that sad face, but it was a face glowing with peace and joy.

A CONVICT PREACHER.

A gentleman arose in the meeting and said that on a previous Sabbath he visited Randall's Island to address the prisoners confined there. On his way he fell into the company of a gentleman who, he at once found, was an intelligent, earnest Christian man, a gentleman of refinement and education. On his way to the Island he made up his mind that he would invite his stranger friend to make some remarks to the prisoners.

"So," said the speaker, "after I had spoken to the men, I invited the stranger to address them. He had not spoken long before many of the prisoners were deeply affected. Many of them were in tears.

"'I know how to sympathize with you,' said the stranger. 'I know how to feel for you. I know what your sufferings are, and how you long to be free. I know, for I have spent six long years of my life in an

English prison. But here you see me now—a professing Christian—a minister of the gospel in the Presbyterian Church—settled over a Presbyterian Church—not lost—but *saved*, just as you all may be, with an everlasting salvation—saved to usefulness and happiness here—a brand snatched from the burning—saved forever.'

"I cannot describe to you," said the speaker, "the power of this strange man's words. They came from the heart, and they reached the heart—*for the man had been there*. He knew it all from his own experience, and the sympathy of such a man moved the men. But there was another chord of sympathy more than all. It was a sympathy with their spiritual wants and spiritual condition, through his sympathy with Christ. He made them feel that Christ was the sinner's Friend, out of prison walls or within them—no matter where the sinner is—nor how great a sinner he is—nor how grievous his transgressions—he has one Friend.

> 'One there is above all others
> Well deserves the name of Friend,
> His is love beyond a brother's,
> Costly—free—and knows no end.'"

"IS MY HUSBAND TO BE SAVED."

"As I was leaving the prayer-meeting," said one, "when I had gone a little distance, a lady came rushing up to me, and exclaimed—'Oh! my brother; my brother. Oh! is not my husband to be saved? I have put in a request that he might be prayed for, three times; and three times this request has been read; and in each case no allusion has been made to my case in the prayers which followed. My husband has not been prayed for. What does it mean?'

"'Well,' I said to her, 'Suppose you keep on praying for him. I will pray for him. I will speak to others to pray for him. We will carry his case to other places of prayer.'

"The heart of this wife was very much encouraged. When I met her again I inquired, 'Is your husband converted yet?'

"'Oh! no, he is not converted; but I believe he will be. My husband is certainly to be a Christian. I feel assured he will be.'

"In a few days I met her again. I asked her—'Is that husband of yours a Christian yet?'

"'Oh! I am afraid not. I have been praying and hoping, and believing. I am so distressed with anxiety for him, that I have had to give up all attention to all household duties. I cannot oversee my house. My hope is in God, and I will trust in *him*, for vain is the help of man.'

"A few days after, I met this same wife again.

"'Is your husband converted yet?' Her countenance lighted with a spiritual, serene and holy joy.

"'Oh! yes, I hope my husband is converted. He came home from his business. He ran to me, threw his arms around my neck, and in rapture exclaimed: Oh! I have found the Saviour, I have given myself up to him, and on the very next Sabbath I am to unite myself to the people of God. I am with you now for time and eternity.'

"'I asked him where he was,' added the wife, 'when he experienced the change.' He answered: In the Fulton Street Prayer Meeting. And this was the first knowledge I had that he ever attended the Fulton Street Prayer Meetings at all. So while I was praying he was going to the place of prayer, where the Lord met him in his mercy.'

"Were I to name him," continued the speaker, "you would all know him, for he is a marked and eminent man in this city.

"Now just mark one thing," said the same voice, "how God, by the Spirit, supported the faith of this humble, feeble believer; and how at the same time He broke her off from all human reliance, that the excellency of the power might be of God and not of man."

A hallowed influence fell upon the prayer meeting. Then how beautifully came in these lines, which were sung with deep emotion:

> "One there is above all others,
> Well deserves the name of friend;
> His is love beyond a brother's,
> Costly, free, and knows no end."

Revivals always bring with them scenes of amazing interest. It is no small event for a soul to come up out of the darkness of sin into the glorious light of the children of God. To bring an alien from the commonwealth of Israel, and a stranger to the covenant of promise, without hope and without God in the world—and from this to become a fellow-citizen with the saints and of the household of God—is a change which is wonderful and incomprehensible. Hence when Christians hear a new-born soul telling its experience of the great change, it is not strange that their hearts should be greatly moved, as they often are in this prayer meeting. A man rises whose voice has never been heard before, and in three or four minutes gives such an account of his religious experience as melts all hearts and brings tears into all eyes. So it often is.

CHAPTER VIII.

UP FROM THE GATES OF DEATH.

"Just in the last distressing hour
The Lord displays delivering power;
The mount of danger is the place
Where we shall see surprising grace."

It is not often that the interest of this prayer meeting has been more deeply intensified than it was by the relation of the following chain of incidents, showing how interesting and surprising is the grace of God in the salvation of men. It is wonderful grace. This was the case of a young man in a good position in a large publishing house in this city. He was about thirty years old, a married man, and happy in all the relations of life. The missionary of the church knew him through years of comfort and prosperity. Years passed away, and we come to a dark place in this man's life.

In the prayer-meeting the speaker gave an account of the wretched life produced by intemperance. The career of this poor sinner is dreadful. He disappeared and was not heard from for some time. He separated himself from his family and from all good.

He was met in Boston by an old friend, who noticed a marked difference in his appearance. He approached him, grasped him by the hand, and said:

"'I am a changed man. I one day got up in the morning, after a night of wakefulness, and thinking over what a wretch I had become, and how wretched I had made my poor wife and children, I resolved to go to the barn, and there all alone to pray that God would take away utterly forever my accursed thirst for rum, and to pray till I felt assured that my prayer was heard. I went down on my knees, and on them I stayed until I had asked God many times to take away all my appetite for rum and tobacco, and everything else which was displeasing to Him, and make me a new creature in Christ Jesus—a holy, devoted Christian man, for the sake of Him who died for sinners. I told God that I could not be denied; I could not get up from my knees till I was forgiven and the curse was forever removed. I was in earnest in my prayer.

"'I was on my knees two hours—short hours as they seemed to me—two blessed hours, for I arose from my knees assured that all of the dreadful past was forgiven and my sins blotted out forever.

"'Oh! I tell you God hears prayer. God has made me a happy man. I left all my appetite in that old barn. In that old barn I was born again; I then and there begun a new and holy and everlasting life of consecration to Jesus.

"'I tell you'—still full of this theme—'religion is a glorious reality: think what it has done for me, a poor, lost sinner. Here I am on my way to the daily prayer-meeting in the Old South. I am happy, my wife is happy, my children are happy. I am a member of the church. I am President of a Young Men's Christian Association. Not one twinge of the old appetite has ever been felt since my meeting with God in the barn.'

"And there we stood in the street in Boston; he was telling of his religious experience of surprising grace, and I a listener to the voice of one who was, when last seen before, a reeling drunkard in the streets of New York. But now he was among the ransomed of the Lord.

"The tears were falling down the cheeks of us both as we stood there with both our hands clasped together, his face all lighted up with gratitude and joy —not the burst of a moment, but the overflow of the well of salvation which was within.

"I have known this man when he was not worth anything to himself nor to anybody else. Sometimes I would speak to him as I met him in the streets, and sometimes I would pass him without a word. All this time of degradation he was sensitive of any neglect to notice him, and well knew what it was for.

"'How about your worldly circumstances?' I asked, as we were parting in the street in Boston—he to go to his prayer meeting and I to go my way.

"'Oh! as to that,' he answered, 'I have to struggle as we all do; but I have this promise, As thy day is, so shall thy strength be. God takes care of that, too. While I am struggling I am always rejoicing in the Lord, and my peace flows like a river, and my salvation like an overflowing stream.'

"This is wonderful—wonderful grace!" added the speaker.

LOST—BUT SAVED.

The following facts given in the prayer-meeting, illustrate what working Christians may do to save those "ready to perish;" for no one could be nearer the brink of destruction than the young man herein spoken of, and after all make good his escape.

This was a young man from Scotland, about twenty-five years of age. He had been blessed with pious parents, and had been early trained in the knowledge of the great doctrines and duties of our holy religion. But yet he lived without God and without hope in the world. He was on a venture for life.

On coming to this city about five years ago, without the assistance of friends, he made many vain and unsuccessful efforts to get into business. Like thousands of young men who roam the streets of this great city for employment, he found the avenues to business all closed against him. Every step he took was into a dark and hopeless future. Every day he must live, and yet the means of living became every day more uncertain. What should this poor young man do? What should become of him? He became more and more desperate and discouraged. Like many others he betook himself to drinking-saloons, and gradually acquired the habit of partaking of the intoxicating cup to drive away his anxiety and cares. He entered upon that down-hill road that leads straight to destruction, and he rushed along the descent with a rapidity of which he was not conscious himself. He was a lost young man.

The missionary of the old Reformed Church found him in the Sabbath-School room one Sunday morning about four years since in a state of beastly intoxication.

Seeing him there, and the children coming in, the missionary said to him: "This is no place for you. Will you be good enough to leave, and not to be seen by these children in your present condition?"

The poor young man got up and staggered out the best way he could. The missionary felt afterwards not a little sorry, because he had dismissed him so summarily, and entirely contrary to his usual custom, without having any knowledge of his lodging-place, or where he could be found. He never expected to see him again. But to his surprise and joy, he saw the young man come into the Fulton Street Prayer Meeting the next day, and he asked prayer for himself. After meeting, the missionary had conversation with him, and inquired—

"From what country are you?"

"From Scotland."

"Had you pious, praying parents?"

"Yes; parents who took the utmost pains to give me good religious instruction?"

"Praying for you from your childhood?"

"Yes; from my childhood."

Then prayer was proposed, and they knelt down, and the missionary commended him to the God of all grace, and begged that God would save this poor sinner, in answer to the prayers of his parents, who were far away, and in answer to the prayers which had been offered for him in the meeting.

The young man proved to have acquired an excellent education, and was possessed of a fine mind. He continued to come to the daily meetings, and at times would arise and ask prayers for himself. He came every day. He was in earnest.

In a short time the case was greatly changed. The pledge of total abstinence had been signed. The sins of a lifetime stared the young man in the face. He was bowed down under a load of sin and sorrow.

The degradation to which he had reduced himself was keenly felt, and the manner in which he had destroyed all confidence in himself was an appalling fact. What should this poor young man do? The missionary kept his case under his eye. He gave him counsel, and urged him to apply to the Great Physician, who alone could give him help and save him.

One day he arose in the meeting and gave a narrative of his case as a poor, lost sinner, and now hoping he had been *saved* through faith in Jesus Christ. It thrilled all hearts, and the conviction was general that this man had passed from death to life.

The next thing demanded was to find him some respectable employment, and encourage him to respect himself, and stand firm to the pledge which he had taken, and to the confession of faith in Jesus which he had made.

The opportunity came, and a high position was in prospect. Meantime he entered zealously upon some missionary work, preparatory to a better place. As in everything he did, he was in earnest, and was gaining the confidence of all.

One day this young man went into a store to buy a pair of boots, and the storekeeper, an old acquaintance, asked him to drink with him. He drank—and fell. His old appetite was kindled in a moment, and he drank and drank again, till he was entirely overcome. His fall was dreadful.

He came to the missionary and confessed what he had done. He seemed to be dreadfully grieved and sorry for what he had done. But the missionary and another took his case in hand, and bade him not despair. A very strong pledge was drawn up, and he was asked: "Will you sign this on your knees?" and, said the missionary, "Will you pray and promise God, most faithfully to keep this pledge?"

He kneeled down, and two with him. He said: "I pray God to help me; and I promise God never to taste the accursed beverage again."

"What shall we do now with him?" said the missionary to his friend. The friend answered: "We must reinstate him, and give him an object and a motive to good conduct, and we shall see him prove himself to be a man?"

He was reinstated. He was made to feel that his Christian friends had not lost sight of him nor confidence in him. He performed his duties to great acceptance on the part of his employers. He continued to advance in the esteem of his Christian friends and in the confidence of the church. He was a changed man after all.

This once *lost* but now *saved* young man, to-day stands at the head of one of the public institutions of the city. The duties of his position he discharges with marked ability. He wields an able pen, and the literature of the day is often enriched by his contribution.

HOPE FOR THE HOPELESS.

A request for prayer was read to the meeting from one there present, who represented his case to be hopeless. He had become intemperate. His friends had given him up for lost. He had given himself over, and he seemed to be doomed to perish. No power but the power of God can quench this soul-destroying appetite for rum, by reason of which his very being was consumed. No tears, or prayers, or resolutions avail anything for a single moment. They are all broken through by this terrible desire for rum. "Will you pray for me to-day in the meeting," says the writer, "that I may be delivered from the power of the destroyer before my eternal doom is sealed and I lie down in a drunkard's grave and a drunkard's hell."

Very earnest prayer followed the reading of this request, in which it was asked that God would give the power, through faith in Jesus, to this poor young man, and by simple reliance upon him, to overcome and resist the temptation, and "bring his soul out into a wealthy place."

After prayer a young man arose and said:

"I have been coming to these meetings about two weeks, and for the encouragement of the young man who makes this request for prayer, I want to ask your indulgence a few minutes to tell you how the Lord has dealt with me. They have been two weeks of the richest experience of the divine goodness and grace. Two weeks ago I was a hopeless drunkard—a poor, lost man I was. My friends had made every possible effort to reclaim me, but with no avail. I had often resolved, with many tears, to break away from the cruel bondage in which I was bound. I took upon myself the most solemn vows that I would reform. What were resolutions and vows before such an inexorable enemy as mine! I could not stand to them a moment. At last I gave myself up to perish. There was no hope for me. I was given up, too, of all the world.

"In this state of despair I went down to the Fishing Banks one day. There I was attracted by the very pleasing countenance of a young man. I knew he must be a poor man, and a fisherman by profession. He helped me to understand the art of fishing. There was a world of happiness in his face. I loved to look at it. At last, out of gratitude for the little favors which he showed me, a perfect stranger, I took out my flask of liquor and offered him to drink.

"'No,' he said, 'I never drink intoxicating drink, and I ask the Lord Jesus to help me never to touch it.'

"I looked at him with surprise, and inquired, 'Are you a Christian?'

"'Yes, I trust I am,' he answered.

"'And does Jesus keep you from drinking intoxicating liquor?'

"'He does; and I never wish to touch it.'

"That short answer set me to thinking. In it was revealed a new power. I went home that night, and said to myself, as I went, 'How do I know but Christ would keep me from drinking if I would ask him?'

"When I got to my room I thought over my whole case, and then I knelt down and I told Jesus, just as

I would tell you, what a poor, miserable wretch I was; how I had struggled against my appetite and had always been overcome by it. I told Him if he would take that appetite away I would give myself up to Him, to be His forever, and I would forever love and serve Him. I told Him I felt assured that He could help me, and that He would.

"Now I stand here and I tell you all most solemnly that Jesus took me at my word. He did take away my appetite then and there, so that, from that sacred moment of my casting myself on His help, I have not tasted a drop of liquor, nor *desired* to taste it. The old appetite is gone, and I tell you, moreover, that I gave myself to Jesus in that very hour, and I received Him as a power in my soul against every enemy of my salvation, and He saves me in His infinite grace.

"I came at once to these meetings. I have been coming every day for two weeks, and oh! what happy weeks. I am delivered through the power of Jesus from the awful destruction which was before me. Such has been the method of my relief."

The young man speaking was known to some in the meeting as belonging to a distinguished law firm of this city.

"WHAT A GLORIOUS CHANGE FOR ME!"

Another gentleman immediately arose and said he had a few words to say to the despairing young man in the meeting.

"I have been two years living by the power of Jesus above; the same evils with which he is beset, and by which I was once surrounded. No man has ever been nearer hell than I have, and yet escaped from it. Years and years I lay at the very mouth of the awful pit. I was given over to destruction by my best friends and by myself. He said, this trying to reform is of no use. It fails so often, that we must believe the failure final.

"One day as I was working in the field to earn a little money to keep me from starving, I took out my bottle, without which I thought I could not live, and I said to some one, for days I have not lived on anything only what I can get out of this bottle. I cannot live so. I cannot live *with* this vile drink, and I cannot live *without* it, and what am I to do? I should like to know that. What is a poor wretch like me to do?

"'Why do you not ask help from God?' said some one. I had never thought of it. It was like life from the dead to cast myself on the help of God. I closed an agreement with Him, by which he became mine and I became His. This was two years ago. What a glorious change for me. What happy years these have been for me. My family are happy—my business prospers. I am now a member of a Christian church. All my relations in life are changed, and all because I depend on God. My love of liquor is gone; all is changed.

"For a time my old companions in drink tried to win me back; but they have long since given it up, and I have won some of them to Jesus. I cannot tell you how happy I am. All this comes by living by faith on God."

This gentleman's voice has been often heard in the prayer-meeting, but until now he had never told the experience through which he had been called to pass, and the dreadful evils from which he had escaped.

SEVERAL REMARKABLE FACTS.

A young man said:

"I was a poor, miserable drunkard. The last voyage I went, I was carried on board drunk. When I came to myself, I began to curse and blaspheme, near the galley, and right off. I was reproved for it by some men standing by. 'Hoot, toot,' said I, 'what does this mean?' 'Means this,' they answered, 'we do not like to hear you take the name of our God in vain.' The amount of it was we had shipped two pious men. When I found this out, I was very much afraid. I was alarmed about myself, and really resolved that I would attend to religion. I wrote to my dear, pious mother about my feelings, and told her about the two pious men in the crew, and sent the letter off. Then my feelings began to grow dull and cold. After a time I got a letter from my dear mother, and that letter made my blood run cold. She told me how glad she was I had pious shipmates—begged me to improve my opportunity—warned me against the awful consequences of grieving away the Holy Spirit. That letter pierced me through and through like a dagger. I never found any peace till I found it in believing in Jesus."

A pious captain arose, and said:

"I am about to go to sea, and my inquiry has been, where shall I get a pious mate. And I have prayed to the Lord Jesus to give me a pious mate. Thank God, the pious mate is given me, and my prayer is answered; and his voice has been heard in the testimonies of this evening. O, who will doubt that God hears and answers prayer. God has heard my prayer."

Another said:

"If any persons had said to me some time ago, and only a short time ago, 'Why do you hang round the drinking-holes and bad houses, and dance-houses? you ought to keep away from such places,' I should probably have told them they had better attend to their own business, in no very innocent language. I should have believed it impossible for me to keep away from such places. I was one who gloried in my shame. But God, who is rich in mercy, and can save to the uttermost all such as come to Him, through Jesus Christ, has been pleased to pardon just as great a sinner as I am, and washed me from my sins in his own blood, and I expect to-morrow to make public profession of my faith in Jesus, and to unite myself with the people of God. I want you all to pray for me."

STANDING ON THE BRINK.

There are many who are scarcely saved, if they are saved at all. They are the many who are ready to perish, and the prayer-meeting makes us acquainted with many of these cases. The following is an example:

"I earnestly request your prayers in behalf of a young daughter who attended a prayer-meeting in upper New York and was induced to appear among the anxious inquirers who requested prayer, but who is now in a very unhappy state of mind, and in a recent letter speaks as follows to her mother:

"'I am more of a hypocrite than ever, and can never expect to be convicted of the Holy Spirit, or to be converted in the future that is before me. How do you think I felt when I read your letter, telling me that you prayed that I soon might rejoice and find peace and light? I felt that your prayers were in vain, and that it were far better had I never been brought into existence than to deceive you as I did—making a mockery of such serious things. But I will do so no longer. If God in His boundless goodness and mercy shall ever lead me to see my sins in their true light, to have right views of his character and to be brought to repentance and abhorrence of my sin, I will gladly tell you. But I feel this will never be. Instead of being nearer I am very much farther away from all that is good, and pure, and true, for God is a God of truth and hates all iniquity and falsehood! Oh, you do not know the depths of sin to which I have fallen! I burned up all my letters I ever received, and thought seriously of drowning myself. I wrote on the slate telling what I was about to do. I used to go down to the creek and stand and think of plunging in, but could not get up the courage. When coming back I would say to myself, 'Why don't you drown yourself and end all this trouble?' This is what I wrote on the slate:

"' *Before you read this my soul will be in eternity.* I write this to say I am in my right mind, and am as rational as I ever was in my life. But I have committed sins of such a character lately, in addition to the sins of my life, as it were scarlet and crimson, which can never be blotted out by the blood of Christ. And I do not want to live on, committing sin and thus treasuring up wrath against the day of wrath.

"' The sins I have committed are, telling such dreadful falsehoods, leading them to believe that I had been convinced of sin by the Holy Spirit and was anxious for my soul's conversion, when it was all a lie gotten up by the instigation of the devil; and by so doing I have trifled away my soul. Misery inconceivable and never-ending is my portion. I know that such a thing as true religion is desirable and will make those who possess it happy, whatever their earthly lot may be; but there is nothing of the kind for me.'"

Such was the letter this poor girl intended to leave behind her. But she could not get the courage to make the fatal plunge into the cold waters of death. She writes to her mother thus, after her purpose of self-destruction had been abandoned:

"'Dear mother, do not give up pleading with God for me. I will endeavor from this time daily to read a portion of God's Word, and will try to pray this prayer: 'O Lord, grant that the Holy Spirit may show me my sins and lead me to Jesus. Hear and answer for Jesus' sake. Amen. I will also go to Sunday school and to the church whenever I can. Your affectionate daughter, 'MARY.'

"'Such, Christian friends, is the state of my daughter's mind. I feel that your prayers, together with my own, may bring down blessings upon her soul.

"(Signed) "'AN ANXIOUS MOTHER.'"

RUNNING TO THE PLACE OF PRAYER.

A young man arose, and said he must beg to state his case. He had made a great effort to get into this meeting, and he had come expressly to ask for the prayers of the assembly. Said he:

"I was in this Fulton Street Prayer Meeting on the fourth of April last; again on the fourth of July, and now I am here again to-day. And I want to tell you how I came to be here to-day. This morning, while I was at my work, my little boy handed me a religious paper. I took it and read awhile. I do not know as what I read had any connection with what followed, but such an overwhelming sense of sin came over me, that all at once I resolved that I would come to this prayer-meeting. I belong in Union county, in New Jersey. I am here to ask you to pray that I may obtain mercy through our Lord Jesus Christ."

Very earnest prayer was offered for him. The leader said he wished to speak, for the benefit of that young man, of a case in Ireland. A young woman was smitten down under a sense of sin. Her minister came to her and said, "Look to Christ, and He will give you peace." "Oh! sir," said she, "it is not peace I want, but Christ." So it is with every sinner. It is Christ he wants. That young man went away rejoicing in hope. It turned out that he had to run three miles that morning to get to the cars in time to come to the meeting.

CHAPTER IX.

THE SEA GIVING UP.

A man who had been for many years on board ship exhorted all to look to Christ, and Christ alone. He had heard of this meeting when he was thousands of miles away. He had been steeped in sin for forty years. He had been overtaken by the Holy Spirit when he was running under full sail upon a lee shore. He had been warned to 'bout ship and claw off before he got into the breakers. Said he:

"I heard the warning, and piping all my hands on deck, related to them all my bad passions, appetites, and sins, and I told them in plain language that they had brought me to the very brink of ruin. *Hereafter* they should all be put down in the hold, and the door be battened down till they were starved to death. They had been near the death of me, and I would be the death of them. I told them I was about to take on a Sailing Master, and He was to have all power on board, and there was nothing He hated so much as such a crew as they. He had promised to help me, and His help meant something. I charged them with being my enemies, and the Great

Captain had promised that they all should be put under my feet. So I bade them farewell, and expressed my hope that I should see them no more forever.

"And now you see me here. I am here for the first time in my life. I have been nine years in the service of my new Master. Nine years ago I could not read, and now I can read as well as most readers. I am trying to do good. I am happy in my work. I have this testimony for Jesus, that He never leaves nor forsakes me. I sometimes forsake Him, but then I soon come back to Him, and I wonder He does not upbraid me; but He never does. As soon as I come back to Him with a sorrowful heart He speaks such words of comfort to my soul, that my heart melts with penitence and love."

The meeting was greatly moved with this old sailor's confession of his faith in Christ.

SAILORS' YARNS ON CHRISTIAN EXPERIENCE.

"Shipmates," said a sailor, "bear a hand and help us in this meeting. I don't know how to tell it short —what the Lord Jesus done for me. He has done a great work—blessed be His holy name—when He washed my sins away. Talk about scarlet and crimson, they were no names for my sins. They were worse than this. I was converted about eight months ago, and oh! how happy I was. Have been ashore some time; have never spoken in this meeting; was four months at sea : and had something to do with, I hope, the conversion of the whole ship's company.

"We had prayers in the cabin morning and evening.

Go where you would over the ship, in the tops or below, you would hear the men singing praises to God. Oh! what a happy crew was that—every man had become a child of God in that voyage of four months. We were all discharged at Valparaiso, but I have heard from many of my shipmates on other vessels, and all are holding out good witnesses for Jesus. Three of them are now in this port; and to-morrow (Sabbath) expect to make a public profession of their faith in Jesus, as their Saviour."

A Norwegian sailor said:

"A short time ago, I went to the Mariner's Church, in which God was pleased to awaken me to a sense of my sins. I found I was a poor, lost sinner. After a time, the Lord was pleased to have mercy on me. As soon as I was converted, I felt constrained to go right home to Norway. I went at once, and I did not leave until my father and mother and one sister were converted. Oh! shipmates, I want to see you all coming to Christ. O that you would come to-night— I know some of you are anxious—come to Jesus now."

Another said:

"I was awakened in the midnight watch. Another sailor was awakened at the same time. We were far at sea. For some time we groped in darkness. Then light came to both of us. Do you think you can know how happy we were? We prayed together—sung together. Oh! what blissful seasons we had. I never knew what happiness was before."

Said another:

"Two months ago, I was in this port, a very wicked man—went to the Mariner's Church—boarded here at the Home—went into the meetings, only to find what a ruined creature I was. But the mercy of the Lord met me, and I felt that I was a pardoned sinner. Went to sea—met with much persecution—but it only drew me nearer to Christ. Have done something in winning others to Christ. Some of my shipmates were converted—some are here now, awakened—don't know what to do, or which course to steer. Oh! that they might be converted to-night."

Another arose and said:

"I am going home to die no more, as we have been singing. To die no more, we must die unto sin, and be made alive in Christ. So I hope I have been made alive. I was—oh, how wicked—in the rum-shops and houses of ill-fame, always when in port. I gloried in my shame. I was the chief of sinners, yet God had mercy. I am to join the church to-morrow —shall be baptized—put on Christ anew. Oh, what reason have I to bless God!"

A young captain said:

"Our last voyage was a blessed one. When shipping my crew, a boarding-house master came to me and said, 'Do you want a crew?' I said, No; my crew were engaged. He said, 'I can give you a crew of pious men.' I looked at him with astonishment. I had known him as a very wicked man. Such men are being converted."

THE YOUNG SAILOR'S COUNSEL.

A young sailor arose. He was evidently a Scotchman by birth. He was deeply impressed, as all could see by his voice and manner, that this was a critical moment; the turning-point to some awakened souls. Said he:

"Will you take a sailor's advice,—a stranger sailor —you who are now deciding that at some future time you will be a Christian; will you take a sailor's advice and not delay your choice another hour, but come now and be on the Lord's side? You cannot possibly magnify the danger of delay. You cannot believe it to be half as great as it is!"

And then he spoke of some of his dreadful experiences of the effects of procrastination. He related the following as coming under his own observation:

"I remember, when in Panama, one of my brother sailors was taken very sick. I had previously, on many occasions, urged him to take Jesus as his guide, counsellor and friend. But his answer had ever been, 'Time enough yet.' That fearful putting off; that delivering himself up to the power of Satan, who was constantly whispering in his ear, 'Time enough yet,' reached its fearful crisis at last. As he lay sick upon his mattress, his writhings and contortions denoted the fever and pain that were within. But the fever of his soul was causing much more anguish than all his bodily ailments.

"I said to him, You need a Saviour now. 'Oh,' said he, 'I have put off seeking Jesus too long.' I earnestly begged him to look at the cross of Christ, and there learn what Jesus had done and suffered, that a poor sinner like him might not perish, but have everlasting life. But he replied, with choking sobs, 'Too late!'—'too late!' 'Oh!' he cried, 'no rest for me. I am going to some place I know not where. Oh! I know not where!' His head falls back upon the pillow. I cried 'Ned! are you dying?' But all I heard was—through the gurgling in his throat—'No rest,'—and my dying shipmate was gone."

Another touching incident he related as intimately connected with his own conversion, bearing upon the danger of delay. It was at his own home. He had a very pious, God-fearing mother, who had never neglected any opportunity which offered to impress upon his young mind the urgent need of seeking a Saviour in his youthful days. But he had constantly neglected to pay more than a passing attention to his mother's admonitions, until one Sabbath morning his mother invited a young girl, a neighbor's daughter, to accompany them to the house of prayer. She replied in a light and trifling manner:

"'Oh! no, I cannot go till next Sunday. I shall

have a new bonnet then; my old one is too shabby.' Alas! that next Sabbath never came to her. On Monday she was taken quite sick. On Wednesday she died. My mother told me, with streaming eyes, as she came home from watching at her bedside, 'Emma is gone; and gone, I fear, without conversion.' This was so sudden, so unexpected, that it woke within my heart the cry, 'What must I do to be saved?'

"And, blessed be God, that cry was not made in vain. Jesus had mercy on my soul. He has been ever since that time the Rock of Salvation. Oh! come to him all you who need the saving grace of a dying, risen Saviour? Will you take a sailor's counsel? Will you come? God is calling you! Come now."

"LAST WATCH ON DECK."

A noble specimen of an old English sailor made his appearance in the Fulton Street Prayer Meeting. He was born nearly eighty years ago. When about fourteen years of age he was bound an apprentice, as cabin-boy, to a Captain Clark, of Salem, Mass.; and when in the West Indies the ship was overhauled and he was impressed into the British service, he being a British subject. He was employed in the British navy. He was with Lord Nelson in the battle of Copenhagen. He now wears, dangling on his breast, a handsome silver medal, given him in commemoration of the victory gained by the Admiral in 1801. It was given him for his courage and bravery on that occasion.

Fifty years ago, he said, he began to preach the gospel to seamen. He originated the first Seamen's Friend Society, the first Seamen's Bethel, and the first Seamen's Temperance Society. All this time, fifty-seven years, he has been an active man-of-war's man, diligent in the service of the Great Captain of our salvation. He gave to those present a rapid sketch of his life, and stirred up the meeting wonderfully by his graphic description of the horrors of war as he had witnessed them on ship and on shore. He was with the British army in Spain, and also in the peace of Paris. He was so moved with the sufferings of the wounded, after a hard-fought battle, that he begged the privilege of devoting himself to their instruction and consolation. He said he had no language with which to describe the scenes which he had witnessed. Said he:

"I have had long a desire to visit America, to which I was on my way when fourteen years old. It seems strange that I, after service in so many wars, and after having been in so many battles, should come and find you in a state of war. If I were to choose my place, now that I am here, I would choose this place of prayer, oh! how earnestly to pray. God is moved by prayer. He alone can direct the whirlwind and still the storm.

"Let us go forth to battle, for some must go—and some must go never to return; but oh! give me this place of prayer if I have any part to act in this matter. First and last, I have been much engaged in offices of kindness among the wounded in battle, and I know all about it,"—and the old veteran stood shaking his head, as if those eyes had seen sights which he did not wish to describe. "It is my last watch on deck," said the old tar—"my last watch on deck. Soon I must go below."

The old sailor preacher wears his honors with humility, being at the head of some of the most important societies in England for the benefit of seamen, and an active leader still in those great religious movements in which British Christians are engaged.

THE YOUNG SAILOR.

The leader, in opening the meeting, said we must not depend upon ourselves in the meeting, nor upon our prayers, nor upon our efforts. We must depend upon nothing but Divine power and grace for answers to our prayers. He illustrated these truths, by the case of a young sailor, who, after his conversion, had been exalted to a higher post of trust and duty. When the first officer of the ship was laid low by disease, he thought there was a good time for him to do something. So he began with great zeal doing something; but he soon found that he did nothing. He looked for great success, but no success came. He thought he could tell his shipmates just how to become Christians. But he found his instructions were thrown to the winds. No one gave heed to them.

At length he told another Christian his disappointment and discouragements. "Ah!" said the other sailor, "you depend on *yourself*, and that is the reason you are disappointed. 'It is not of him that willeth, nor of him that runneth, but of God who showeth mercy.'"

A SAILOR'S LETTER TO THE MEETING.

It was dated at San Francisco, September 20th, and stated that he had shipped on board the Nonpareil, at this port, on the 16th of April previous. He found to his great joy, on going on board, that there were five pious sailors on board. They began with a prayer-meeting every day, and they maintained it all the way to San Francisco. Not a word among the ship's company was ever heard said against it. In his letter he says:

"Within one month from the time I landed in New York, I hope I was converted. I came to New York in the ship Radiant from Calcutta, in which Rev. Mr. Bronson, of the Assam mission, was returning. Through the instrumentality of the pastor of the Pierrepont Street Baptist Church, Brooklyn, I was humbled and brought to the foot of the cross. I think your prayers for me were answered. I hope you will all remember us in your prayers. We have had a prayer-meeting every evening on board, and they have been a great blessing to our souls. Not one on board ever passed an unbecoming remark on us. If we had not the right spirit this could not have been. One of my young friends is going to join the Baptist Church in San Francisco. Pray that he may be kept faithful."

A sailor followed in a very remarkable prayer, full of grateful praise that the Lord had given him a pious mother, who never wearied in praying for him.

The leader took his seat, and a verse of a familiar hymn was sung, after which a young, earnest-looking man, a Norwegian, arose and said:

"I feel thankful to be in port again, thankful to meet you here. Some few months ago, when here, I was invited to go to the Mariner's Church. I went only to find and feel myself to be a poor, lost, ruined sinner. How wretched I was. I did not know what I had been all my life, an enemy of God. I was borne down with sorrow. But it pleased God to show me how I might be saved by Jesus Christ, through faith in his name. I felt that my sins were all forgiven, and I found great joy and peace in believing in Jesus. The first thing I did, after my conversion, was to go straight home to Norway, to tell my father and mother what a Saviour I had found. I did not leave Norway till my father, and mother, and one sister was converted. Oh! what cause I had to rejoice."

"Another sailor said :

"I was awakened at midnight, in the midnight watch, another sailor was awakened at the same time. After awhile the Lord had mercy on both of us, and we were converted, and then, Oh! what happy seasons we had! What times of prayer together! How we comforted and encouraged each other. Oh! shipmates, come to Jesus. Come to Jesus! I see some here I want to have come to-night. Come to Jesus now."

A cheerful, encouraging verse of a hymn was sung, with great earnestness and animation. A young sailor said :

"The lightnings have been playing around us, in the shower this afternoon, and they made me think of the manner of my own conversion, far, far, at sea. In a thunder-storm I was struck with lightning, and was taken up for dead. As they were carrying me along the deck, I heard the mate say : 'Poor fellow, he is gone.' I was conscious, and knew all that was said and done. I said to myself 'Where will I go to?' In a moment, all the acts of my wicked life passed in review before me. It seemed to me there was not one thing I had ever done, that did not come up to be looked at. It was an awful sight. I thought hell was not far off, and go there I must. I was dropping right into endless wailing. They revived me, but I had been too near eternity to be any longer indifferent. I fled for refuge to Christ. It was five years ago. I have stood up for Jesus everywhere, on land, on sea, ever since. All this time I have been praying for my father and mother, that they might be converted. And to-day is the first good news I have had. I got a letter to-day that some of my dear friends are converted. Glory be to the name of Jesus. I know that God hears and answers prayer."

Another young sailor said:

"Ten months ago I was in this port. I was very wicked—very wicked in everything that such as I plunged into, while in such a city as this. I went to meeting at the Mariner's Church. I was convinced what a great sinner I was, and I was going to an awful judgment, and an endless eternity. I went to sea, and I have been eight months away. I have come home a new creature in Christ Jesus. I expect to put on Christ afresh to-morrow, in the holy ordinance of baptism, and be received into the church. Three of my shipmates were converted on this voyage. There are others of my shipmates who are here—they don't know what to do—they want religion they say, but they do not know how to set about it. They do not know what steps to take. Oh! that they would be persuaded that they have nothing to do but to come to Christ. Oh! come at once to Christ. He alone can do you any good."

After a verse of affecting singing, another said:

"When I was awakened, the Lord gave me plenty to think about. I was pretty well burdened I can assure you. It was a grievous load. I was a drunkard—a bold blasphemer—a poor ignorant despiser of Jesus—a man steeped in crime. I had enough to think about, full enough to think about. And when the Lord rolled off the burden from my soul, and set my captive spirit free; oh! it was such a salvation, I had enough to talk about. When a new song was put into my mouth, I had enough to sing about. I *did know* next to nothing. All my vanity was gone. I could not read a word, but I determined I would learn to read the Word of God. I got a New Testament, and I began in that. I learned my letters, and then I spelled out the words. I prayed to the Lord Jesus to help me to learn to read his holy Bible, and I believe he did. I can read it now as well as any of you. And oh! what riches do I find in God's blessed Word to the children of man. Treasures richer than mines of solid gold are there unfolded to my grateful heart."

THE SEA CAPTAIN'S STORY.

He said he had followed the sea for more than forty years, and he was now over sixty years old. He had been commander of a ship, and he considered himself, some time ago, a man of no little importance. He came home from sea, some months ago; and he was urged by a pious, anxious sister to go to the Fulton Street Prayer Meeting. He refused, point-blank. He told her he would not go. She still urged him; and somehow, she one day found he had gone, and he, most unexpectedly to himself, found himself in the meeting. He came to see what sort of a meeting it was.

"But," continued the captain, when narrating these events, "I had not been long in the meeting before I got a dagger in my bosom, which I could not haul out again. You have no idea how small I became in my own eyes. I had not the least idea a man was such a little insignificant creature. Why, I could have crawled away anywhere. I could have crept in a knot-hole. I went about with a heavy heart for about three months. I really did not know what to do. I had a load on my heart, and I did not know how to get it off.

"I was speaking to a friend, one day, to whom I unburdened my sorrow. Said he: 'Why, there is only one way for you. You must come to Christ just as you are!' 'What,' said I, 'go to Christ right off-hand—sinful as I am?' 'Yes,' he said, 'just so. You cannot make yourself any better. He does not require it.' You cannot imagine what joy those few, few words gave me. I believe my heart embraced Christ just while he was talking to me. I tell you, I felt that it was good news to me, that I could go to Christ just as I was. What happy seasons I have seen since then! I want to persuade all who hear me to come to Christ just now, and just as they are. I went about with a heavy heart for months. I did not know that Christ would receive me as soon as I was ready to receive him. It was good tidings to my weary soul, when I was told to go right to Christ at once; and every day I go to him, and keep going, and he gives me all I need."

CHAPTER X.

PARENTS AND CHILDREN.

A few facts are given to show the power of parental and filial faith and love. When one of the meetings was about half through, the chairman announced a personal request for prayer. He said he had been informed that an individual was in the meeting in a state of great religious anxiety, who desired the meeting to pray for his conversion. This individual proved to be a gentleman of high professional position in the city—being a physician and a professor attached to one of the Medical Colleges in New York.

He continued to come regularly to the Fulton Street Prayer Meeting, and promptly at the hour of 12 M. he would be seen entering the place where prayer was wont to be made, and through the services paying the most diligent attention. At length, one day he arose and asked the meeting to pray for him, a poor, blind sinner, who needed the illumination of the Holy Spirit to lead him to seek salvation through our Lord Jesus Christ. He confessed that he knew not how to get relief.

A very deep sympathy was awakened in the meeting in behalf of this awakened, religious inquirer, who did not know what to do. Tracts were given him, which he gladly received. Spiritual counsel was given him, and his case was often remembered in prayer in the meeting.

At length the light began to dawn upon his mind —feebly at first—but it was the true light, so far as we could judge, that enlightens every sinner's soul who is brought to believe in Jesus. At first, hope was feeble and light was dim. But it rapidly grew brighter, and hope grew stronger. That dreadful load of anxiety was gone, and the lately despairing, lost sinner was found sitting at the feet of Jesus, and rejoicing in the great salvation with joy. When asked how he was getting along, he would speak with great modesty, but with a good degree of confidence of the great change.

Yet there were times when he would be at a stand, and could hardly persuade himself that all was real. It was so great a change that he was afraid of some kind of illusion of the mind. He would say that such a sinner as he had been, to be found depending alone on Jesus Christ, and believing in him unto eternal life, as he hoped he did, was beyond his comprehension. He sometimes doubted whether he was not deceived about his own convictions and consciousness. But as time passed on he became more assured.

One day he arose and requested leave to tell how the Lord had dealt with his soul, and had led him out of darkness into marvellous light. He began by saying:

"I have been one of the most wicked of men. After wasting a fortune on myself, I met with a calamity which will go with me to my dying day. I resolved that I would retrieve my broken fortunes, and have a name and fame in the world. I worked hard night and day to make myself a master in my profession. To some extent I succeeded. But I was never happy. I was always miserable—no man more miserable than myself. For ten years I thought I had been somewhat earnest on the subject of religion. I regularly attended church. I had the Bible read to me. I really thought that I was seeking religion all this time. But in this I was deceived. I was in darkness and spiritually blind.

"When of late it pleased God to open my eyes to see what a sinner I had been, the sight of myself and my sins were terrible. I would wake in the night groaning with mental anguish. My wife would ask, 'Where is your pain? Can you not do something for it?' I would tell her, 'My pain lies too deep for any human hand to reach. It is internal, and no medicine will cure it.' So I was oppressed with a load of sorrow.

"Finally I seemed to be told, as if a voice spoke to me, 'There is one sin greater than all—the sin of unbelief. You do not believe the Bible. You do not believe in religion. You are an infidel. And when I examined into my own heart, I found it was all true. I really did not believe in the Bible—in religion—in Christ—in anything. When I found the accusation which was laid against me was all true, the sins of which I seemed to be guilty, and which were so enormous, those sins which before so distressed me, dwindled down into insignificance, and the sin of unbelief towered up like a mountain above all others.

"At length I began actually to rejoice in my infidelity. I really began to think I had not been such a great sinner as I had accused myself of being. I was glad to find that I had been thus mistaken in my estimate of myself, and there I rested for three days. I do not know what you will think of this phenomenon, but I call it a spiritual paralysis. My system sunk down under the load.

"But at length conscience began to assert its power. Those sins which had sunk so low as to be out of sight, rose up against me again with gigantic force. Oh! I cannot tell you what a dreadful state of heart and mind I was in. I bore a burden which I could not shake off with any power of my own. I tried everything. I could do nothing—praying—reading the Bible—nothing gave me any relief. Can you imagine a man more miserable than I was!

"At length I became convinced that all my infidelity must be given up—that infidelity was really no remedy for my condition. There was no remedy but in Jesus Christ. More and more deeply this truth was fastened on my mind. I saw in Jesus Christ a remedy for my distressed and distracted condition, and to him I went for relief.

"Now it seems to me the change is just as great a miracle as the change in Saul of Tarsus. I am a miracle of grace. Sometimes I can scarcely believe that simply believing in Jesus is all. And yet it is all. I I have grown stronger in my faith in him. I believe in him with all my heart. I believe in the Bible—in it all, from Genesis to Revelation. It is sometimes said that the studies of our profession lead men to admire and adore the wisdom of God. So they ought. All I have to say on this subject is this: If any of your sons intend to enter on these studies, let them first make their peace with God, and become true Christians, or I am afraid they will never do it.

"Now, if any one should ask — How did you become anxious on the subject of religion? I have to make this answer: I had a pious, praying Presbyterian mother—a devoted mother—one of the best women that ever lived. I believe that mother's prayers have been following me these long years. I believe that her prayers and your prayers have been answered. There are no prayers like the prayers of a mother.

"I am aware that the earnest sympathy of this meeting has been drawn out towards me. For this I feel very thankful. Hereafter I can only be here on Saturdays, as our medical lectures commence to-morrow. But on Saturdays I shall endeavor always to be here. I have made up my mind to one point—always to stand up for the Lord Jesus Christ. If I must sacrifice my duty to him or my duty to my profession, my duty to my profession shall go. I will be before my classes a follower of Jesus, and everywhere make known my faith in him. Thanking this meeting for their kind interest in my behalf and for the prayers which have been offered here in my behalf, I must ask a continuance of your kind remembrance in prayer, that the Lord will ever keep me and uphold me with his hand."

Earnest prayer followed that the Lord would keep him with His holy keeping, this new trophy of His victorious grace.

Another case of wonderful conversion was that of a young man. He came into the meeting, as he said, accidentally, but as he now says, providentially—out of mere curiosity. He had an unfair opinion of the meeting. He looked upon it with no small disdain.

As he was leaving, a friend put into his hand one of the little cards of the American Tract Society, and he went on to the store in which he was employed. That little missive called up his attention to the subject of religion. He was soon in deep distress, and found rest to his soul only in coming to Christ. The same man that gave him the card, a stranger, went into the store, to call on another friend, and found that this work had been wrought in the young man's heart; and all by this humble instrumentality, in the hands of the Spirit. This young man, too, had a praying mother.

A gentleman in the meeting said that among all the conversions which are now taking place, almost every day, among seamen in this port, nine out of ten of them have praying mothers. This had been ascertained by special inquiries made to that point.

AN INFIDEL IN THE MEETING.

A young girl came to the meeting, and was observed to be weeping. Some one inquired into the cause of her weeping. "Oh!" said she, "if my father only knew of my being here he would not let me come. And I fear I cannot come any more."

"Why not?" asked the inquirer.

"Oh! my father is an infidel, and he does not believe in these places of prayer. He would not let me come."

The next day she came again, and, coming up to the gentleman who had spoken to her on the previous day, she said, with a smiling face:

"Father is here. I told him I had been to the Fulton Street meeting, and, instead of saying I should come no more, as I expected, he said he would come himself and see what sort of a meeting it was—and here he is."

Now he comes every day, and has become deeply

interested, and there is strong hope that he will soon become a Christian. He says that he cannot avoid coming. The daughter is already rejoicing in the hope that she has been born again, and is really a new creature in Christ Jesus. And now she is praying with great earnestness that her father may be brought into the fold of the good Shepherd. He acknowledges that he is not without deep religious anxiety. He believes that this is truly a place of prayer. After a time the light began to dawn on this poor man's heart. He was drawn and influenced to put his trust in Christ and make public confession of faith in Him.

"WHO TURNED DOWN THAT LEAF?"

"I was sent for (said a gentleman in the meeting), to visit a young lady in a very anxious state of mind. I have always felt the importance in talking with such, to keep to the words of Scripture—the word of God—and rely on that, as the fire and the hammer, to break the flinty heart in pieces. I was invited, on entering the house into the parlor. I had never seen the individual whom I had called for. But while waiting for her to come in, I stepped to the table, and took up a neat little Bible, and opening it, I found a leaf turned down, and the corner of the leaf pointing to this particular passage, and I thought there was something significant about it. The passage pointed to was this: 'Be not afraid; only believe.' When the young lady entered, after the usual salutations, still holding the little Bible in my hand, I inquired—

"'Who turned down that leaf?'

"'My dying mother,' she answered, with much emotion.

"'Well, have you trusted, according to these words, in the *Author* of these words?'

"'Never,' she replied.

"'Not in Jesus?'

"'Not even in Jesus?' and a tear was seen falling down her cheek.

"'Could you do anything better?'

"'I presume not.'

"'Why, then, not believe?'

"'How can I believe, when I do not believe?'

"She looked perplexed and troubled. I knew that the Holy Spirit was moving on her heart, and again inquired—

"'Would not Christ have felt insulted, if those to whom he addressed these comforting words had said, how can we believe, when we do not believe?'

"'No doubt of it,' she answered.

"'Is it any less insulting for you to say it, than for them?'

"'Not the less—perhaps the more.'

"'Here is this leaf turned down for a purpose, by your dying mother: what purpose do you suppose it was?'

"'That I might read and obey these words:' and the tears were falling fast.

"'These words are the path, and this leaf turned down is the finger-post, pointing to the path in which she wished her dear daughter to walk, when she was dead and gone. Now will you walk in it?'

"'There was a solemn pause. She trembled violently as she stood beside me. At length she said—

"'I will.'

"'Will what?' said I.

"'I will not be afraid, and will believe.' She said it solemnly and with great emphasis.

"'Let us pray,' said I; and we dropped upon our knees. I thanked the Lord Jesus for these precious words, and for the good resolution of my young friend, that she would not be afraid, but would believe; and implored him to lead her heart and mind to place all confidence in him as a Saviour able and willing to save.

"We arose from our knees, and I felt that the great decision was made. I have called upon her since, and I always find her rejoicing in Jesus."

We do not believe that an hour of prayer has ever been held, in all these fifteen years of prayer, in which there has not come requests for prayer from mothers for their unconverted children.

These requests are always very touching and move all hearts to pray. And very—very often the news comes that prayer has been answered. Often men arise in the meeting and ascribe their salvation to God in answering the prayers of praying mothers.

THE DYING WOMAN'S TESTIMONY.

She had been taken out of a miserable abode in Gold Street, in a sickly condition, to the Hospital. She failed day by day. Her mind was in spiritual darkness. From the lips of the good missionary she received constant instructions in the great things connected with her salvation. The clouds and the darkness cleared away, and the light of the Sun of Righteousness shone into her heart " with healing in his beams." She had, at length, firm, unfailing, and unwavering hope in Christ. To him she devoted her all, and waited patiently for his appointed time to call her to himself. She had two lovely children under the care of a devoted sister, who had cared for them with a mother's tenderness while the mother lay sick in the Hospital. Since the sickness of the mother, this sister had become hopefully pious. The dying woman had a husband. He was still impenitent.

The dying hour had come. The little family had gathered around her dying couch to hear her last words, and receive her last tokens of affection. The missionary was there. The whole kneeled around her. The missionary, taking one of her dying hands in his, and the hand of the husband in the other, said:

"Now, what is your dying testimony?" addressing the wife.

"Nearing the shore."

> "Jesus, lover of my soul,
> Let me to thy bosom fly."

"I make this language mine from the bottom of my heart."

"What is your request for your husband?"

"That he become a child of God at once, and give himself to Jesus."

"What for your children?"

"I commit them to the keeping of my Heavenly Father."

And in a few more minutes she was gone—gone to her eternal home. So they are going. And the great day alone will reveal how they go—from whence they go—to what they go.

"Blessed are the dead who die in the Lord."

CHAPTER XI.

ANSWERS TO PRAYER.

Every chapter and every page of this history furnish answers to prayer, but a few specific cases out of thousands will be read with interest. One of the speakers said:

"One week ago to-day, I was in this meeting, and heard read a request that you would pray for the conversion of the two children of a widow—a son and daughter; I knew the family. The reading of that request was followed by the prayer of a clergyman, who was so fervent that I felt in my own soul that that prayer would be answered. When I went home, I found that daughter of the poor widow in my parlor. I invited her to go to a prayer-meeting in the evening with me, to which she readily assented.

"'Where is your brother,' said I.

"'I don't know,' said she, 'I invited him to go to the prayer-meeting with me, to-night, and he refused, I do not know where he is. But I suppose in his usual haunts of pleasure.'

"We went to the prayer-meeting. We had been there but a few minutes before the brother came in and took his seat. He and the sister were so deeply impressed by this meeting that they resolved to come again the next night.

"They did come again the next night, as proposed, and there the son of the widow resolved that he would go home and commence family worship and that son and daughter are now rejoicing in the pardoning grace of God.

Another case was mentioned by another individual. He said he had a little time ago presented the case of a Roman Catholic lady, who came into these meetings out of mere curiosity, but who heard while here things, which she never heard before; who said she would be very thankful if you would pray for her. She was deprived of her sleep at night by reason of her great anxiety of mind—had no confidence that she was a Christian—but greatly desired to become one. Said the speaker:

"Now I come to ask you to join me in thanks to God for the conversion of this Roman Catholic lady. She is rejoicing with great joy in the belief that her sins are pardoned. And when I asked in whom she relied for all her hopes of salvation she said, 'I have no confidence in confession, no confidence in the church—I trust in Christ alone. I hope to be justified through him.'"

A NEW CONVERT.

Said a young man lately converted:

"It is but two weeks since I found an interest in

Christ. I am but two weeks old as a Christian, I am impressed with the deep conviction that I am not my own. I have been bought with a price: even the precious blood of Christ. I have begun in earnest to do the duties of a Christian. I have conversed with and urged my best friend to the duties of a religious life, and I know him to be anxious on the subject of religion. I am anxious you should pray for him. I am anxious for his conversion. I hope we shall live a religious life together, shall run up together the shining way, and be associated together in the great work of leading sinners to Christ. I have also a brother for whom I request your prayers. He is the only one now left, whose case is without hope, in our family. If he were brought into the fold of the Good Shepherd, then we all should be the sheep of his pasture, Pray for him.

"And if there be a young man here having no, interest in the Saviour, let me say, the pleasure of this world were as much to me as to any young man: I had as much to enjoy in them, and as much to enjoy with my associates as you. And yet I must say, that in the past two weeks I have enjoyed more real, solid, substantial happiness, than in all my life before. What I before enjoyed I count as nothing.

"I count it less than nothing, in comparison with what I now enjoy. Surrounded as I was with everything that could make life a pleasure, I had as much to give up as any one. And long, long was the struggle maintained in my own heart between giving up the pleasures of sin for a season, and submitting myself at once and forever to the service of God. But at length the contest was ended, and I yielded to the unspeakable claims which Christ has upon me. I exhort my young friends to come to Christ. His yoke is easy. His burden is light. I had tried everything but religion; I feared religion would strip me of all happiness, that it must be *endured* for the sake of gaining heaven. How mistaken I was. It is heaven below to be a real Christian, and it will be always heaven, and by-and-by heaven completed.

Said another:

"I am to leave you to-day. I have been written to and begged, and entreated to come home by my parents and family, who had cast me out, and who had told me that I should never more come inside of their doors. But by my letters home, and the Lord's blessing on them, my father and mother and one sister have been converted, and now they say they will welcome me home with exceeding joy. But my heart is grieved—my heart is grieved!" he exclaimed, as the tears rolled down his cheeks,—"at leaving this place so dear to me, where I learned to love Jesus. The very floor of this room, on which we have so often knelt to pray to Jesus, and on which we have stood to speak of Jesus, is near to me. Oh! how can I part from this dear sacred place, and my much-loved brethren and sisters? Oh how can I say I shall never come here any more? How can I say I shall never see your faces any more? And his tears flowed afresh, and every heart was melted. "But," rallying, he said, "It will be only a little while and on the floor of gold, in the heavenly temple, I shall meet you, and I shall not have to say farewell. Oh! brethren and sisters meet me there; and let us strive to bring all our dear Roman Catholic friends along. Poor people! how little they know the way. I promise you, before I go, I shall not be idle. I shall not be still. I shall never be ashamed or afraid—if God will only help me, and I know he will. He always stands by me. My Saviour seems always near to me, and I ask you to pray for me that I may speak for him."

Who would have believed that this man now speaking was a persecuting hater of the prayer-meeting a little time ago, but such he was.

Then another arose, who had been one of the most desperate and hopeless cases; a Roman Catholic and a bitter hater of the truth; one who had stood on the opposite sidewalk and hurled stones in at the window. He spoke rapidly, and told what the grace of God had done for him. He was a scoffer, miserable, ignorant, drunken and debased, and thought he was as good a Christian as anybody, because he sometimes went to confession and got his sins pardoned, and sometimes went to church, and hated Protestants with all his might.

"Now I don't hate anybody. I pray in my family. I have plenty of employment. I am always happy. All I want now is that my wife will come with me, and she will.'

Another spoke in very broken English. He said we might not be able to understand him, but the Lord Jesus could understand him. He went on to speak of his conversion. How bigoted he was when he was a Roman Catholic; how ignorant; how the Holy Spirit had enlightened him; how his heart was all glad for joy. "I love to pray. I love to read my French Bible. I love this meeting. I love poor sinners. I love to tell them of Christ." So he went on speaking, some of which we could not understand.

A VOICE FROM CHICAGO,

Said a man springing to his feet:

"I am from Chicago. I attend a daily prayer-meeting there very much like this. It is animated with the same spirit of holy prayer and faith. In that meeting, too, poor sinners are converted. Let me tell you of one case.

"It was the case of a Jew. He was observed in the meeting to be in great distress. He was surrounded by a few Christians, after the exercises were over, who endeavored to arrive at the cause of his trouble. They found it was all about his soul—all about his sinful self.

"They undertook to read to him the third chapter of John and the account of the Saviour's conversation with Nicodemus. With great impatience he said, throwing up his arms, 'Don't talk to me about *that man*'—'don't talk to me! I don't want to hear about Him.' All this time meaning Christ.

"Then they went down the page till they came to this verse, 'As Moses lifted up the serpent in the wilderness so must also the Son of Man be lifted, that whosoever believeth on Him should not perish but have everlasting life.'

"The poor Jew started up at once and said, 'Is that there!'

"'Yes,' he was answered, 'it is here.' 'Let me read it myself,' he said, and he was directed to the place. All at once he shut his eyes and put his hands over his face, and the hot tears were streaming through his fingers; after a pause he said, 'I see it! I see it'

"'What do you see?' said a brother.

"'I see it! I see it!' he answered with more emphasis than before. 'I see it! I see it all now!'

"'What do you see?' was again the inquiry.

"'I see Jesus upon the cross,' he said, 'the Son of Man lifted up, that whoever believeth on Him shall not perish, but have everlasting life,' and I can believe on Him as the Messiah that was to come and save his people from their sins.'

"It was a hearty and full confession of faith in Jesus Christ as the Saviour of sinners. Christ the way and the truth and the life. The poor Jew is to-day rich in the faith of Jesus."

"MET ME AT THE GAMBLING TABLE."

A young man, apparently twenty-six years old, arose. It was easy to see he was greatly agitated, and embarrassed.

Said he:

"I have come here often, determined to speak, and I could not. I have compelled myself to get up and tell what Jesus has done for me."

The young man's eyes filled with blinding tears, and he struggled to control his voice, as he proceeded to say:

"I had a pious father and mother. My mother especially prayed much for me. With strong crying and tears she implored Divine mercy upon me. I have been very wicked—few so wicked as I. I neglected all duty, and ran riot into all forms of sin. I spent much of my time at the gambling-table. Some time ago the Holy Spirit met me at the gambling-table. How mysterious are his ways. Who would have thought it? But it was so. I was hit with an arrow from His quiver. I found no peace till I came a trembling sinner to the feet of Jesus. I have now become a tiller of the soil. I have wanted to tell you how I found Jesus. He heard my mother's prayers when the Holy One took me away from the gambling-table."

THE PRAYER OF FAITH.

"The great need," said a clergyman, "is more faith." 'According to thy faith, so be it unto thee.' is just as much the rule and promise now as it was in the days of our Saviour. As God's method of rewarding the faith of his people was always the same, and as it was often necessary to look back for our encouragement in duty, at the present, he proceeded to relate an incident which occurred thirty-two years ago, in a village in this State.

A revival of religion commenced in the place, with great power, operating upon the hearts and minds of a large portion of the population. It so happened that a man of large influence and intelligence, was offended, in the very beginning of this work of grace, with the work itself; and he set himself in strong opposition. This was a matter of great regret and sorrow among Christians.

Many were discouraged, because this man seemed to have such a control over the minds of many. It happened that at the meeting of four or five of the elders and leading members of the church, at the house of the pastor, there came in a very pious, godly minister, and the course of this man of commanding influence came up for remark. "Why not pray for him?" said the strange clergyman; "why not pray for him, here and now?" So they all knelt in prayer, and prayed in turn, and it was noticed that this strange clergyman was very deeply moved, for a man whom he never knew, and had never heard of till that day, a perfect stranger to him. But he knew that he stood in the way of the salvation of souls, in opposition to the work of grace which was then going forward, and his soul was burdened. The season of prayer was continued. Much prayer was offered. At length the strange clergyman said he felt an assurance that their prayers were heard and answered.

Now, said the speaker, just notice what God was doing to hear and answer those prayers. At the time they were praying, the Lord directed to the store of this man, a clergyman, who was a relative by marriage, but who was a stranger to the circumstances before stated. He engaged in religious conversation with this opposer. He noticed that as he proceeded his words sunk deep into his heart. The tears were standing in his eyes. He urged his immediate compliance with the requirements of the gospel. He submitted on the spot; acknowledged his opposition; confessed his sin, and avowed his determination to be on the Lord's side. That man was a truly converted man, as his after life showed. He proved by a life of untiring devotion to his Saviour, the reality of the "great change." Here was the prayer, and here was the answer to prayer.

STORY OF A CONVERSION.

These are nearly the words of the narrator:

"About two years ago, just after my own conversion, God blessed me in the conversion of some of my friends. I also was deeply interested in the conversion of some others who were yet without Christ. So I resolved to select some who were most intimate with me, and make them the subjects of special daily prayer.

"I took out my little diary, and wrote down four names. Under these names I wrote as follows:

"'I do this day resolve, before my God, to remember these persons at the throne of grace until they are converted. Oh! God save these souls, and give me great faith, for Jesus' sake.'

"After I had written down those names, I looked at the last and said to myself, 'This is a very gay, careless young man. I have some influence over the other three, but not much over this one. I have not faith to pray for this soul, and praying for him will be mocking God.'

"But I could not forget those words, 'According to thy faith, so be it unto thee.' I thought, 'How shall I meet that at the bar of God?' I could not take that name from my list for prayer. I did pray earnestly for him.

"I was surprised and gratified to see this young man come into one of our meetings for prayer; and from his appearance he seemed to be very much interested. We talked and prayed with him. We urged him to give all up to Jesus. But he felt that he could not give up all—his companions, his social enjoyments and worldly pleasures. He sat in the same pew with me.

"My mind was wrought up to an agony of prayer. I prayed that Jesus would give an evidence of His love, by calling that young man to manifest his concern for his own soul by asking for prayer for himself.

"I said, 'My dear Jesus! I have prayed for this soul with all the earnestness of which I am capable. I have testified of Thy love, here in this room. I am almost discouraged. I have not received any answer to my prayers. How can I pray for these other three, with unshaken faith believing? Now, dear Lord, if this young man does not seek his own salvation, how shall I believe the other three will seek theirs? Ought I not to feel my heart is wrong before, and that I have no faith.'

"Finally a quiet came over my mind, and I said:

"'Dear Lord! I can believe—I will believe. I will trust Thee with all my heart and soul.'

"Soon an opportunity was given for all who desired the prayers of God's people to manifest it by rising up. In an instant my young friend was on his feet, his whole appearance betokening the most intense mental anxiety. I felt like shouting out, 'Glory to God,' my joy was so great.

"The next morning I met him, and asked him how he felt. He answered, 'It is all decided—all decided.' He had decided for Christ, and hope and heaven.

"These names were written on the 10th of February, 1869. And before the close of the month the most unpromising of the four was converted, and himself was engaged in urging sinners to come to Jesus, finding in his own experience that it was a blessed work, blessed service!"

The narrator did not tell what had become of the

more promising *three*, for whom he felt it was much more easy to pray, and for whose conversion he had faith.

THE MERCHANT'S FAITHFULNESS REWARDED.

A merchant was very anxious for the salvation of the clerks in his store. He was one of a firm, and his partner in business was not a pious man. He said to his partner one day, that he wished to attend the Fulton Street prayer-meetings. His partner coldly answered that he could do as he pleased, but *he* thought it was best to attend to business *first*. The merchant, however, went into the meetings. He became greatly interested, and deeply impressed, and felt that this was a place of the Holy Spirit's presence and power. He continued to go daily, and daily his interest increased.

He said to his partner, one day, that he wished the clerks of the store could go to the prayer-meeting. "As you please," answered the partner, "but for *my* part I think we ought to attend to business *first*. Business is business, and should be attended to in business hours." The merchant made no reply, but asked the bookkeeper if he would go to the prayer-meeting with him.

"I suppose I must," said the bookkeeper, in a very careless and indifferent manner. It was as much as to say, if he went at all he should go to please his employer. But he went, and he continued to go, till he was awakened and converted in a short space of time. Then there were two who were interested in the salvation of the two remaining clerks in the store. One of these he wished to invite to go to the prayer-meeting. So he said to his partner:

"I am very anxious for the salvation of the young men in the store. I am also anxious for yours. It is now an important time with us, and it ought to be improved. Will you go to the prayer-meeting?"

The partner replied,—"You can, of course, do as you please. But for *my* part, I think we ought to attend to business *first*."

"Are you willing that one of our clerks should go each day?"

"I am willing you should do as you please about inviting them, and they as they please about going. But my own opinion is we ought to attend to business *first*."

"Seek first the kingdom of God," said the merchant.

"That will do very well for some men, and for some seasons. But business has its claims and its time; and in its hours I believe it is *first* to be attended to."

The conversation was here dropped. The merchant invited one or the other of the remaining clerks to accompany him to the prayer-meeting, and in a little while he had the unspeakable joy of seeing both of them brought into obedience and love of the truth as it is in Jesus. All the clerks in that mercantile house are now hopefully pious.

The merchant says that his business has never been so prosperous since he and his clerks have begun to attend the prayer-meetings. It was a city merchant who was speaking. He said that a few days ago a country merchant came into his store to buy a bill of goods; and while he was looking over the memorandum of articles which he wished to buy, the man remarked—"Since I was here before, I hope I have become a Christian." He was asked how that was, and in reply he went on to say that six months ago he was in the city and came into the Fulton Street Prayer Meeting. He said that he went out of that prayer-meeting fully determined to seek the Lord until he should find him. He, and others who had been into the meetings went home to pray and seek earnestly of God that he would pour out his Holy Spirit. And the Lord heard and answered prayer, and more than two hundred had been converted in the place (Ovid, N. Y.), and the country merchant who came into this meeting an unconverted man is now a new creature in Christ Jesus.

CHAPTER XII.

POWER OF PRAYER.

A gentleman of Virginia spoke of prayer as a power. God had placed it in our hands. How little we use it! Does He not hold us responsible for the use of it? If He gives sight, are we not responsible if we shut our eyes and refuse to use the power to see? The speaker continued:

"So of the power of hearing—the power of speech—are we not responsible for the use of these powers? God gives us the power of prayer. What countless illustrations we have, coming to us daily, of the power of prayer. Here, in this meeting, we are told of this wonderful power. A father enters his closet, where there is no ear to hear save the Omniscient ear; or a father and mother bow down together before the family altar; and then we hear what is done away up in the mines of California—what no power on earth could accomplish but the power of prayer."

In Williams Valley, Pa., more than one hundred have been received into the churches. In Milton, in the same State, there are reported more than one hun- and seventy-five hopeful conversions. To one church, in Pittsburgh, there have been more than one hundred added to the number in communion, and one hundred to the church in Jacksonville; and more than twenty towns, besides the above named, are now enjoying the blessing of the power and presence of the Holy Spirit, in securing the salvation of a great multitude of souls. So much have we heard from one State. Something similar to this may be said of every State in the Union.

The most powerful revivals we have heard of are in Kansas, where, in some prayer-meetings in the large towns, hundreds rise for prayer. In nearly all the larger towns there are great numbers turning to the Lord.

In a village in New Jersey, a powerful revival of religion had begun. We called upon the pastor, anxious to learn the facts and the origin of the revival, and the proximate causes which led to it. About forty had been added to the church at their last communion, and as large a number at the one which is now approaching, are expected to join.

The pastor himself gave us accounts of wonderful conversions, showing what the Lord had done. It was manifestly the work of the divine Spirit, for no special means had been used. Everything had been most discouraging. The pastor had been prostrated by ill health, so much so as to feel compelled to ask a dismissal from a people all united in him and he very much attached to them. They had very reluctantly agreed to join him in asking that the pastoral relation might be dissolved. Now what was the origin of this wonderful work of grace?—for it came in great power. The pastor's wife wrote a letter to the Fulton Street Prayer Meeting, begging them to pray for the outpouring of the Holy Spirit upon the church and congregation, and especially upon the young in the Sabbath-school and out of it. She particularly asked that her five sons might be remembered in prayer that they might be converted. The window in heaven was opened, and the rain of heavenly grace descended. Three out of those five sons have been converted, and many of the youth of the place, also many adult persons and heads of families.

The spirit of prayer had been awakened in the heart of that pastor's wife—perhaps, too, in the heart of the pastor—for he was about leaving, as he supposed, a beloved people, for whose spiritual good his heart yearned. We are sure it was so, for he pointed out the corner of his study, where, on his bended knees, he was accustomed to pour out his soul to God in earnest prayer; and often his wife was in prayer at the same time.

Meantime the pastor's health so improved that he was able to leave his house and go to the house of God and preach, one forenoon—a Sabbath; also to attend the church prayer-meeting. In the first inquiry meeting which was held, it was found that several had been already converted, with whom no conversation had been held. God was going before the people. This was the fulfilment of the promise, "Before they call I will answer, and while they are yet speaking I will hear."

SPIRIT OF GRACE AND SUPPLICATION.

Said an old minister, rising to his feet:

"I am glad that we prayed for the recovering from his long sickness of the Rev. Mr. Spurgeon of London. I do not know that our earnest prayers for his recovery had anything to do with his getting well. I, however, believe our prayers were answered, as I believe many thousands of others were which had been put up in his behalf all over the world. I surely believe that that great and good man has been raised up in answer to prayer. And I hope we may still pray for him, for his perfect restoration to health, and for his long-continued usefulness to the Church and to the world. Few men have ever spoken to so many by the living voice and by the printed page as Mr. Spurgeon, and there are thousands now in glory who have been won to a blessed immortality by his instrumentality; and there are thousands on their way to heaven, who have never seen his face or heard his voice, who will be found to have received their first deep religious impressions from some portion of his published works, or his spoken words as reported.

"I am now reading for the third time his 'Evening by Evening,' and I cannot tell you with how much profit to my own soul. When Mr. Spurgeon came from his sick bed into his meeting—a meeting for prayer of more than 2,000 present—with a staff in one hand and leaning on the arm of a friend with the other, the whole audience were melted into tears. He said the one great lesson he had been taught on his sick-bed was his ingratitude for the mercies which had been bestowed upon him. He did not know how much he had enjoyed till he had been laid down *so low* that he could not help himself."

It was a minister who was speaking, deeply affected himself, and moving the hearts of all to deep sympathy as he closed with an earnest prayer for the great London preacher.

A PRAYING TELEGRAM.

God is very faithful to His promise, and we must have faith in His words and believe that He will do just what He says He will. We cannot philosophize about or explain it. Here is an example of this method of answering prayer, as related by one in the meeting:

"When we were in Switzerland my daughter was

taken very ill, so that the doctors despaired of her life. I felt the need of sympathy and help in prayer, and I made up my mind I would send a telegraphic despatch to this meeting, where I had so often united with you in prayer. I wrote the despatch and was prepared to send it, when all at once there was poured out such a joyful faith and confidence in God on me as I never felt before in all my life. And I fell on my knees in devout thanksgiving for the assurance that God gave me that He had heard and answered our prayers, for we had prayed for that dear daughter's life. There lay the telegram ready to be sent. There I was waiting and praying. In less than half an hour my wife came into the room and said, 'There is a change for the better in our daughter;' and the telegram was never sent, though I believe the writing of it had been the prayer that God answered."

The gentleman who is speaking now is a clergyman of the Reformed Church, living a little way from the city, and is the pastor of a village church. He began by saying the power of this meeting can never be known, and proceeded to relate the following incident: A Sabbath-school teacher of his acquaintance attended the late fourteenth anniversary of the noon prayer-meeting, and was deeply interested and affected by what she heard. She went home, resolved to pray for the conversion of her seven scholars. She did so, and it was not long before one of them gave her heart to Jesus, and in about a week the other six followed her example. This was the result of a purpose formed in that anniversary meeting, known only to herself and God. This was the beginning of a work of grace now going forward in his congregation, and for the advancement of this gracious work he solicited earnest prayer.

THE MEANS OF A REVIVAL.

Said another in the meeting:

"I have been in a great many revivals of religion, and I have never been in *one* that did not have in it the main features of the great revival at Jerusalem. As then, so now; Christians must be of one accord in one place. They must pray for the outpouring of the Holy Spirit. They must keep on praying till they are filled with the Holy Ghost. There comes, with this inspiration of the Spirit, an amazing and mysterious power, so that the feeblest means become clothed with a majesty and energy utterly inexplicable and indescribable. It is a force that is irresistible. It overcomes opposition. It makes its way directly to the conscience and the heart. What it is we cannot define. It is 'power from on high.' It is the Holy Spirit in the believer, acting within us and by us. It varies in degree, but not in nature. It often goes from heart to heart in a meeting for preaching or prayer. The great revival preachers of the first ages had it. Peter on the day of Pentecost had it, when three thousand were converted and added to the Church in one day. A century ago preachers had it— Wesley, Whitfield, Edwards, and the Tennants. And all these combined could not tell what it is. It defies explanation or definition. All we can say about it is, that it is a power and it comes in answer to prayer. And without prayer it does not come. It cannot be assumed. It cannot be imitated. Under it, sinners cry out in agony and say, 'Men and brethren, what must we do?' Men in all ages in the Church have been clothed with this power: men and women, parents and children; but in a special manner, preachers of the Gospel. Harlan Page, in his walks of usefulness in the city of New York, carried this power with him. So I might say of James Brainerd Taylor, and many others who preached the word with power, whether they said much or little, or whether they spoke to one or many.

"I once knew a man who was all night long on his knees in prayer for a stout unbeliever, that he might believe. It was a time of wonderful revival. As soon as morning came, he thought he would go and talk with his unconverted friend, and endeavor to lead him to Christ; and when he got where the unbeliever was he could not say a word, and turned and went away. And this going away was the means of the man's conviction and conversion. He knew why the man of mighty prayer could not speak—that it was because he was overcome with his own emotions. This alarmed him, and was the means of leading him to Jesus.

"Christ promises to endow his people with this power, and he keeps his promise just as he keeps the promise to give the Holy Spirit to them who ask Him. I have heard men preach in 'the demonstration of the Spirit and with power.' I have seen whole congregations melted down under the voice of the minister, when, not the voice, but the Spirit melted them. A generation ago, in the time of great revivals, I once heard Dr. Lyman Beecher preach in Philadelphia. It was in one of the largest churches in the city. It was at the time of a mighty outpouring of the Holy Spirit upon the churches. The service was at night, and the great edifice was packed. His text was, 'Thou art not far from the kingdom of heaven.' His object was to show how God by His Spirit drew men toward it, drew men near it, and how easily they might step into it and be forever saved. He preached with remarkable unction. He pictured the condition of the sinner before conversion and after conversion; set forth what he was, but had no right to be—not a moment longer. He showed what he ought to become; that he should not remain for a moment longer far from the kingdom of God, but enter it at once. His sermon was simple and easily apprehended. He poured out the truth in a mighty torrent. In the latter half of the discourse he was more than himself in setting forth what Jesus had done, and what He was ready to do, in helping sinners to enter the kingdom of heaven. His eloquence was full of persuasion and urgency. He showed what a faithful, loving Saviour we have to believe in and trust; and as Jesus was persecuted, crucified and slain for our offences, and had risen again for our justification, the whole audience was moved with the deepest emotion, and many sobbed aloud. No words can do any justice to the scene, as he urged poor sinners to come to Jesus on the spot, and decide the 'vast forever' question now.

"It was the time of the great decision with many, and many were transported that night out of the kingdom of darkness into the kingdom of God's dear Son. What was the secret of this man's power that night? He was preaching under a mighty baptism of the Holy Spirit, and his words were clothed with unction and with power—power from on high. We must have this spirit and this power. We pray in vain and labor in vain without it."

WAS IT IN ANSWER TO PRAYER?

Said a speaker in one of the meetings:

"We speak of the life and the restoration to health of the Prince of Wales. There is a vast amount of skepticism about the whole subject of prayer, and especially answers to prayers, even among Christians. They are too prone to feel, though they may not say it, that 'these things just happened so.' Did they just happen so? Would they have happened at all if there had been no prayer for the life and salvation of the Prince of Wales? Would he have come up from that bed of sickness, nigh unto death, if not only British Christians, but American Christians and Christians of all lands, had not poured out their hearts to God, in earnest prayer, that the life and salvation of the Prince might be given to him and to the British people, for the sake of the honor and glory of God, he being made the instrument of promoting the eternal life and salvation of the vast population of the British realm. No one man living can do so much for the promotion of the gospel as can he, if he lives to be the future king of England! It is not strange that there should be for him such universal prayer. It would be strange if no prayer should be offered for one whose prospective position will give him power to do so much for the cause and kingdom of our Lord and Saviour Jesus Christ.

"For myself, I believe that, in this case, God has heard and answered prayer. I do not believe that the recovery of the Prince 'just happened so' as to seem to be an answer to prayer. No! no! We can see that God's hand is in this recovery, and we cannot but believe that for some great purpose God has raised up one who, when he comes to be the head of a great empire, may use his power in honor of him who is King of kings and Lord of lords. I believe we have not seen the end of answered prayer, but that a thousand times more is yet to be revealed. The time is coming when kings shall become nursing fathers, and queens nursing mothers, to the church of Jesus Christ; and may the Lord hasten the day."

PRAY MORE—PRAY MORE.

Rev. Dr. Plummer, of the Theological Seminary, at Alleghany City, near Pittsburgh, stood near the door, being able to get only this stand-point, and said there was a man standing with his finger upon the pulse of a dying man, while he was continually crying out to those around him, with difficult, but earnest entreaty, "Pray more! pray more! pray more!"

And as his pulse was sinking, and becoming more unfrequent and feeble, he gasped out with his expiring breath, "Pray more! pray more! pray more!"

The speaker continued:

"There is everything around us that continually exhorts us to pray more. When the tender and touching requests for prayer were read, I looked around upon these faces, and I could see here and there a tear stealing down the cheek, as if you felt the appeals which were thus made to you—each of which is saying, '*pray more! pray more! pray more!*'

"Three men and a boy went into a coal mine, one hundred miles west of where I live, and, soon after entering, the earth near the mouth fell in, and cut off all possibility of escape. All the men of the neighborhood were aroused, and they worked day and night, for fourteen days, as hard as men could work, one gang relieving another; and so they worked on, with all possible energy and dispatch, determined to get out the bodies of the three men and the boy—dead or alive—in the soonest possible time; and the language of the whole effort was, pray more! pray more! pray more! Well, they got them out, all alive.

"Yet we are surrounded by men, underneath whom the fires of an eternal hell are burning; and how can we be idle, or do so little? Sinners are perishing from under our eyes—from out of our houses—from these streets and alleys—going down to the gates of everlasting death, and everything cries out to us, in heaven, earth, and hell—'pray more! *pray more!* PRAY MORE!'"

PRAYER OF A YOUNG MAN FOR A YOUNG MAN.

A young man arose in the back part of the lecture-room, and, with great earnestness, made his appeal for prayer for one with whom he had become providentially acquainted. He had been to Albany, and was waiting in the depot building, to come home to New York in the down train. The train, he said, went off and left him sitting in the depot. He felt provoked that the train should leave without giving sufficient notice to passengers. As there was no help for it, he had to walk some distance to take another train, and get down by another road; for he felt that he must come to New York.

"So," continued the speaker, "I started on foot, and now found myself walking by the side of another young man, who said to me:

"'Did the train leave you?'

"'Yes,' I answered.

"'Well,' said he, 'it left me too; and I have often been left here in the same way, and have been obliged to go over to the other road to get down.'

"I learned, on talking with him further, that his mind was religiously awakened, and all the way on that walk, of over three miles, I was trying to urge him at once to come to Christ.

"On leaving him, I handed him a tract which I had happened to put in my pocket, as I was leaving home. I had never read it, and knew not what it was.

It was the prayer of four words: '*Lord: Show me Myself.*' I asked him to read the tract; I presume it was a good one, as it was published by the American Tract Society. He promised to read it, and we parted. As I had another of the same kind, I sat down in my seat after I had entered the car, to read the tract I had given away to a young man. I felt there was a providence in it that I should have been directed to read the tract and to give one of the same to that young man. It is followed by another prayer: '*Lord: Show me Thyself.*' The whole is a narrative tract of the conversion of a young woman by means of making use of these two prayers. So I ask you to pray for this young man. Some of his friends had been killed in the late railroad catastrophe. And this had been made the means of his awakening."

IN HASTE FOR PRAYER.

A young man entered just before the closing exercises and said:

"I must speak. I have come fifteen miles to get to this meeting, and when we landed in the depot, I had but fifteen minutes to get here. I have come from an anxious pastor and an anxious church for the prayers of this people, that God would pour out His Holy Spirit upon them. We have been holding nightly meetings, but the blessing seems to tarry. Our pastor seems discouraged. I want you to pray for us, that the rain of the heavenly grace may descend upon us, and if you pray I know it will."

In this same service, a clergyman said he came here for prayer some days ago in behalf of a church and people in New Jersey. The Lord was pouring out His Spirit in great power, and many had been converted. They began their meetings with the Week of Prayer, and had continued them from day to day ever since. Continued prayer was asked that this glorious work of grace might go on and spread into all the region round about.

Another clergyman arose and said:

"I know it will rejoice your hearts when I tell you of what the Lord is doing in some of our out-stations. At Charlottesburg, N. J., there is a marvellous revival of religion. Hundreds have been hopefully converted. I want you to pray for the continuance and spread of this glorious work of grace. I asked you to pray for this weeks ago, and I believe that this blessing comes in answer to prayer."

Not a day passes that we do not hear of some one in the meeting in a state of deep religious anxiety. A young man has just been on his feet asking prayer on his own behalf. As he closes, a note is read from some one in the room: "One who is present, and whose heart God has touched with the power of His Spirit, desires the prayers of Christians here present, that God would grant him renewing and sanctifying grace, and make him feel more and more his need of a Saviour."

On *one* day, more than twenty requests came in from pastors and churches for prayer for the outpouring of the Holy Spirit upon them with great power. Some gave notice that protracted religious services had been begun, and prayer for the Divine blessing was asked.

A speaker said :

"It is impossible to shut our eyes to the evidence that God is coming in His glory to bless the churches. Who stirs up this desire for the 'Promise of the Father' to be realized ? Who urges us to pray for the Holy Spirit but those whose hearts have been touched by His grace. We should rejoice at these tokens. We should hail them with gratitude and joy. We should welcome the duties to which we are called, and enter upon them with alacrity. We all have work to do. Let us do our work, and work while it is day."

Another speaker said :

"Four years ago I solicited your prayers in behalf of a young lady who was given up to die, but I believe her health has been perfectly restored in answer to prayer."

The following remarks were also made:

"For ten years I have been a slave of intemperance. The pledge was signed, physicians applied to, friends gave their advice ; but it was all of no use, I fell, because I depended on myself. The first Sabbath in this new year I went to church, more to while away an idle hour than anything else; but while there I was met by the influences of the Holy Spirit. I was enabled to give myself up to God in Jesus Christ. I pledged myself to Jesus to forsake every evil and false way. I asked His help against my evil appetite, and He has helped. I declare to you, I have no craving for the accursed thing. I stand in the strength of Jesus, and only in His."

The speaker insisted there was no hope or help for a reformed man but in Christ. A man must have a change of heart in order to stand in safety.

CHAPTER XIII.

RELIGIOUS ANXIETIES.

A young man arose in a late meeting and said that until within a few days he had been in great distress of mind. He had often and often written his own requests for prayer, and had come in, heard them read, and listened to hear how they would be remembered in prayer. At length he was enabled by the ever-blessed Spirit to see that he was depending on this meeting, and not on *Jesus*, and he betook himself at once to the foot of the cross, where he found, as he hoped, that peace which passeth understanding.

Conversions are frequent in the meeting. Persons stay after meeting for conversation and prayer, and make themselves known. A case in point is that of a young man who, after introducing himself, said he had been a professor of religion, but he was satisfied *now* that he never had part or lot in the matter. Though living outside the city he was often in the meeting, and had been here thrown into great distress, so that there was no comfort for him. He was directed to the Lamb of God who taketh away the sins of the world. He seemed to go with great reluctance. He said, "*Will you pray for me?*"

HOPELESS PROFESSORS.

Not a meeting passes but hopeless professors of religion bring their requests for prayer, not unlike the following:

"Dear Friends—I am a professor, but have no hope in Christ; have never been converted. Now I want you to pray for me, not only to-day, but at your homes and in your closets. Ask God to give me His Holy Spirit, to enable me to sorrow for the past, and to exercise faith in the present. Ask Him to enlighten my dark mind, and help to never despair of His mercy."

Here are the touching words of another in a similar state of mind:

"Christian Friends—Do you ever pray for me? My requests have been sent, oh, so many, many times. But I am still in darkness and sin. My heart is very hard. I cannot sorrow for sin. I cannot believe. I cannot make a resolve even to strive against sin. I do not appreciate God's love, nor the love of Jesus. I cannot exercise any of these feelings. I would like to offer my tribute of gratitude for deliverance, but cannot. Wont you pray for me? I am a professor of religion. Must I perish? Does Jesus hear and pity, and yet send no relief?"

These are sad cases, yet it is better to be alive to the truth than be dead to it. Such persons are very apt to be deceived in regard to themselves, and to write bitter things, when their very words show that they are not insensible.

A gentleman who addressed the meeting said he did not think we prayed enough for the young—for the little children. He spoke as follows:

"Children have not only tender hearts to receive impressions, but they also have hearts that take strong hold on their parents, and little children have a power to do good to their parents, which we ought to consider.

"Let me give you an example of this, which came within my own knowledge. There was a family in Williamsburgh, consisting of a father and mother, and two children—the eldest a daughter, the youngest a son.

"The father of these children was never in the habit of going to church. The mother would go, taking her little children with her. The father would stay at home, or go elsewhere. The persuasions of the wife were used in vain to induce him to go to the church or the prayer-meeting.

"One time, his little daughter said to him: 'Father, why do you not go to meeting, the same as mother does?'

"'Oh! go away,' said the father, 'and do not

bother me about going to meeting. I do not want to go.'

"On another occasion, the little boy said to him: 'Father, why don't you go to meeting with mother, and sister, and me?'

"'Oh! go away, and do not tease me about going to meeting,' said the father.

"Then his children got hold of him—one by one hand, and the other by the other hand—and said: 'Father, do come with us to the prayer-meeting.'

"'Oh! go away,' said the father, 'I do not want to go to the prayer-meeting.'

"This he evidently said with an effort. They left him very reluctantly, as he must have seen, and went off by themselves to the prayer-meeting. What did that father do? He could not rest. He could not forget what his children had said to him, and how they had urged him to go with them to the prayer-meeting. He was troubled in his mind. His conscience smote him with repeated rebukes for thus turning against the requests of his children. So he took up his hat, passed out into the street, and made his way to the prayer-meeting. It was to a young men's prayer-meeting, which he knew was held in a certain place, into which he made haste to enter.

"The Spirit of God so wrought upon him that he soon rose up in great distress of mind, and asked the meeting to pray for him. The meeting did pray for him. After the meeting was concluded, some of those young men went with this now thoroughly-awakened man into an upper room, and there they continued in prayer till this man yielded up, in sweet submission, to the claims of the gospel, and by repentance for sin, and faith in the Lord Jesus, laid hold on the hope set before him.

"He went home to his house, with the sense of forgiveness, and rejoicing in having found the Saviour—a changed man. How mysterious are the ways of God's redeeming providence! That little boy, whose kind words overcame the hardness of his father's heart, spoken with childish simplicity and anxiety, now sleeps in the grave. He died at the tender age of six years. But, young as he was, he accomplished a most important mission in his brief earthly existence—that of being instrumental in bringing his father to the feet of Jesus."

One day, after reading the account of our Saviour's apprehension, trial and crucifixion, a young convert, who was evidently very much affected by the narrative, arose and said:

"Perhaps some of you heard with *horror* the rejection of Christ when they said, 'Away with Him—away with Him!' For thirty years I said that same thing when Christ was proposed to me as the Way, the Truth and the Life; as the willing, ever ready, Almighty Saviour; my conduct and my heart said, 'Away with Him—away with Him.'"

The speaker's voice fell to a hushed and almost inaudible tone, struggling for utterance. Every heart was moved, for the audience could plainly see and feel that his heart was melted within him. He continued:

"It is but a few days since I gave in my adhesion to Jesus, and embraced Him as my Lord and my God, and could say, 'Whom have I in heaven but Thee?—and there is none upon earth that I desire besides Thee.'"

His words extended through not more than one minute, and then he resumed his seat, two verses of the hymn being sung:

> "I lay my sins on Jesus,
>   The spotless Lamb of God;
> He bears them all, and frees us
>   From the accursed load.
>
> "I bring my guilt to Jesus,
>   To wash my crimson stains
> White, in his blood most precious,
>   Till not a stain remains."

SUCCESSFUL EFFORTS.

A speaker said:

"Two weeks ago, I asked your prayers for an intemperate family. The following Sabbath I spent two hours in this family, and persuaded them all to give up the intoxicating cup and sign the pledge of total abstinence. Last Sabbath my heart was full of joy at seeing the mother making profession of her faith in Christ."

A young man stood up in the meeting. His voice was a strange one as he related the following incident:

Fourteen years ago, in the time of the great

revival, he was a clerk in a store in this city. His employer induced him to go to the Fulton Street Prayer Meeting, where he was almost immediately brought under the power of the Holy Spirit, and, in process of time, converted. He went to the meeting to find out what it was like, and found out that *he* was like one condemned to die the death eternal. He sought and obtained forgiveness. He had reason to rejoice that he never could or never did shake off his convictions until he had obtained an interest in the Lord Jesus Christ. From the day that he found peace he never neglected opportunities to win souls to Christ. From the hour that light dawned on his spirit he cast all his worldly cares on Jesus. He had long been a resident of the West, and had been much prospered in worldly things. God had given him influence and a heart to work, and he had not labored in vain. He had made it a rule to seek first the kingdom of heaven, and God had kept His promise in bestowing all other things.

Said another speaker:

"I was riding in a street car in the evening, when a gentleman touched me on the shoulder. It was a distinguished lawyer I had set out to see on that morning—now more distinguished than ever; high not only in his profession, but in public life. He asked me to call at his office the next morning. It was a good sign, for by this time he knew my business. I went. He read to me an article he had written for the local paper in favor of a venerable pastor, of whom he had become a friend and supporter. His conversation showed serious impressions; but he was absorbed in many and important worldly affairs.

"At a short distance an evangelist was laboring with great success. With this old minister I attended the services, and he engaged the evangelist to come and preach for him the next Sunday evening. It was with some hesitation he consented to it as an experiment. The indications of that evening would probably decide his course. I was there. After the sermon the preacher cleared two of the front seats and requested any who felt interested in salvation to occupy them. No one stirred.

"It was a new thing in that community, where a revival of religion could hardly be remembered by anybody. In vain the evangelist explained, and urged, and argued.

"Right behind me sat the two daughters of the eminent lawyer, accomplished young ladies of the highest social position, of course. I turned about and said to the oldest one, 'Are you a Christian?' 'No sir,' said she, 'but I wish I were.' 'Then why didn't you go forward?' 'I would if anybody else had.' I turned to the youngest and asked the same questions, and got similar answers. She would have gone forward if her sister had. 'Now,' said I, '*you* would have gone if anybody else had, and *you* would go if your sister would. So, now, according to that you can both go.' Both the sisters rose at once and went forward. Ten other persons immediately followed their example.

A young man was assisted to stand up, and said:

"I am a poor, miserable sinner, a ruined, undone sinner. I want to be a Christian, but I don't know how to become one. I wish I could find my way to Christ, but I don't know how. It is because I don't know, that I don't find Him! I wish you would pray for me. O! pray that I may be converted. I am in great need of help from Jesus, and I don't know how to get it. I have tried and tried, but it don't do any good. The load is all on me yet. I can't live under it. I cannot cast it off. O! do pray for me. Pray that a poor, ruined sinner may be saved."

He sat down, and leaning on the back of the seat before him, burst into tears as prayer was offered.

THE SKEPTIC.

A veteran lay missionary, a plain man, rose to state his experience in testing the promises of God. Said he:

"I was visiting in the neighborhood of my early home for a few days. Finding myself at leisure in the early morning, I said to myself: 'Now you are not going to hunt, nor fish to-day, you might as well go to work just as if you were at home.' I I thought I would not pick out an easy job, but would take up the hardest one on my mind, and that was to go and see a gentleman of very high standing and ability, a lawyer, whom I had never faithfully urged to repentance. I felt myself weak for such an interview, but I thought of the promise: 'Them that honor me I will honor.' And that promise I resolved to test.

"On inquiring for the gentleman at his office, I found he was not in. The gentleman who told me so, however, said he could attend to the business just as well. I told him I was afraid not. But he said he must insist upon it, that he was his partner, and wanted very much to do the business. I thought I would let him try. So I told him what I had called for, admitting that he was as much concerned in it as his partner, and hoping that he still thought so himself. He answered promptly:

"'I do. I have felt the deepest interest in the subject for more than a year—so much so that I have attended prayer-meetings and lingered about until everybody was gone, and the lights were out; but nobody ever said a word to me about religion. I have about concluded that there is nothing in it, or there is nobody that cares for me.'

"At this moment a gay young fellow drove up to the door, and burst into the room. He wanted to know if the lawyer was ready for 'that ride.'

"'Not now,' said the lawyer. 'Sit down.' He sat down and went on talking. Pretty soon he edged his chair in between us. I laid my hand on his shoulder, and said to him: 'What I have been saying to this man is just as applicable to you as to him.'

'"Perhaps so,' said he. 'But I am a skeptic.'

"'A skeptic! How long have you been a skeptic?'

"' Oh! a number of years.'

"' Well, has it done you any good?'

"' I don't know that it has.'

"' Do you expect it will do you any good?'

"' Can't say I do.'

"' Well, then, if it has never done you any good, and is never going to do you any, you would not suffer much loss by giving it up, would you?'

"' No; but the difficulty is to get rid of it.'

"' Do you really want to get rid of it!'

"' Yes, I do.'

"' Let me test that.'

"I drew a total-abstinence pledge from my pocket, laid it before him, and said:

"' Will you sign that?'

"He was all excitement from liquor at the time. He took up the paper and read it carefully through, and considered it well. Then he took the pen from the table and signed it. He was getting away from skepticism faster than I expected. He next took a card out of his pocket, and copied the pledge on it, and returned it to his pocket.

"His friend looked on with perfect amazement, deeply affected, and signed the pledge also. It was a time for prayer. We went into an inner room, and turned the key. Before we came out that young man had given his heart to God. As I bade him good-morning, he laid his hand on his heart and said: 'I never felt so in all my life. I don't know why it is or what it means.'

"' Why, how do you feel?"

"'Oh! so strangely peaceful; so perfectly happy.'

"Not long afterward I heard that this young man was studying for the gospel ministry. He is now a settled and very useful pastor.

"As for the lawyer who attended to my business, a few days ago I saw an account of a sermon preached in some neighboring locality by this same partner, lawyer, and judge. I felt satisfied that he was attending to my business."

STRUGGLING WITH TEMPTATION.

One day after the leader had read the 34th Psalm, in which occurs this promise—"They that seek the Lord shall not want any good thing"—as soon as a proper opportunity occurred, a man arose and said:

"There was a time when the question of my salvation was just reduced to a matter of dollars and cents. The naked question was whether I could afford to become a Christian. I had been for a long time under conviction of sin. I knew I must perish if I should die as I then was. I thought I was anxious to be a Christian. I had been an ambitious young man—ambitious to be rich;—I had fair prospects of becoming so. I saw at once I must make great sacrifices if I became a Christian. I must give up all my cherished plans and schemes. Giving up all these, I knew not how much more was involved. I saw that I might be poor all my days, instead of being rich, and *how* poor was more than I could tell. The adversary assailed me just in this way:

"'You are doing very right to give attention to the subject of religion. It is a very important subject. But you are doing very wrong to make the sacrifice you must to become a Christian; it is unreasonable. You cannot afford it. No one has a right to throw away his blessings. Wealth is a blessing, and you are discussing the question of being poor all your days, when you have every advantage for becoming rich. Be religious if you will, but by all means be rich; and then with a contented mind you can afford to be religious.'

"At the same time the words of Jesus rang in my ears and knocked at my heart: 'He that will not forsake all that he hath cannot be my disciple.' 'If any man will come after me, let him deny himself and take up his cross and follow me.' 'How hardly shall they that have riches enter into the kingdom of heaven.'

"The devil said, 'You do not quote the Scriptures correctly. It is hard for them who *trust* in riches to enter into the kingdom of heaven. You can have riches and not *trust* in them. You are not called to make a beggar of yourself all your life long in order to go to heaven. This would be very unreasonable; and you are never required to do anything *unreasonable* to get to heaven. Be religious if you will, but by all means be reasonable. Do not make a fool of yourself and in your folly throw your blessings away from you.'

"I knew that Christ required me to give up all for him. I knew that I could not have my own way in the matter of salvation. There I hung, just on that hinge—balancing the question whether I would be rich and be without salvation, or whether I would be poor and have salvation.

"It was a dreadful struggle, and Satan helped me into trouble all he could and made it seem hard. I thought I was willing to give up all dishonest and wrong ways of getting riches. But why should I be called upon to give up honest ways of seeking and obtaining the good things of this world for the sake of Christ? That was the point of the struggle.

"It was when I was in just that state of perplexity that my eyes fastened upon that 10th verse of the 34th Psalm—'They that seek the *Lord* shall not want *any good thing.*' This settled the matter with me. I waited upon the Lord, and have not wanted any good thing since."

A young man said:

"I was called to stand beside the bed of death. It was that of my mother-in-law. Her friends, even her own children, could not bear to see her die. They would not be any nearer than the next room. I was in that room alone with the dying. We all have a terror at death. But sitting there and watching the progress of the destroyer, the Lord called my attention to my own condition. I thought what would become of me if I should die? I felt that I should be lost forever. I had no escape from this, but in coming to Christ. I came to Him in a short time. I told my wife we must pray in our family. We began with the Lord's prayer, which we and our two little children repeated together. Now she, as well as myself, is rejoicing in hope. My home is now a happy one."

'When prayer had followed for the last young man who had spoken, that he might be kept steadfast to his new life, to which he had devoted himself, and be made useful among those with whom he was daily employed, there was a pause, and another young man said he had a praying mother, and a praying father. His father had labored for forty years in the missionary field, and then went to his rest. Much prayer he knew had been offered for him. All his friends were praying for him, and he knew that many remembered him at the throne of grace. He had been in a state of great religious anxiety, and it was only a week ago that he hoped that he had found a Saviour. He continued:

"Ministers tell us in their sermons how easy is this coming to Christ. Christians tell us how easy it is, and yet we know nothing about it. I was anxious to come to Him. I resolved upon doing much toward coming. I was going to do many good things, as I supposed. In the morning I could lay out much that I would do through the day. At night, when looking over the day, I found that I had done absolutely nothing. I was no nearer coming to Christ. Then for another day, I would resolve upon duty again, only to find, at night, that I had gained nothing. So I wearied myself with my efforts; all the time, as I supposed, trying to come to Christ but not *coming.*

"So about a week ago I went to Christ in prayer, and told Him all about it. I said, 'Oh! Lord Jesus, I am desolate. I can do nothing. I come to Thee to do all. I give up all to Thee. I want to be allowed to come to Thee, just as I am. I want an interest in Thine atoning blood. I want to be washed from all sin. I want to be taken into Thy service. I want to be wholly Thine, to devote myself to Thee.' I cannot express what a joy came into my heart, in the consciousness that I had really now been accepted of Him. I had really found Him. I found Him when I did nothing else but come to Him just as I was. It now seems easy to come to Him. We must do nothing but come."

SYMPATHY IN RELIGIOUS ANXIETY.

A young lady read an account of the Fulton Street Prayer Meeting, and it was the means of causing her to resolve that she would send to the meeting a request, asking prayer for her immediate conversion. That request came. It stated that she had been in anxiety for more than six months, and she most earnestly begged the meeting to pray that she might believe in the Lord Jesus Christ with a faith which is unto salvation. This was the substance of her request. She stated, moreover, that she had been encouraged to believe and hope that God would answer prayer. She promised that she would also pray for her own salvation. In a few days another communication was received from the same young lady, saying she had found how blessed it was to put her trust in Christ.

In that she also requested prayer for two sisters and a brother. Soon a third letter was received, saying that her brother and one sister were converted, and begging continued prayer till the remaining one should be brought into the fold of the Good Shepherd.

The first letter was suggested by simply reading an account of how God hears and answers prayer in this meeting, and she was encouraged to hope the same might be true in regard to her. Whose prayers were answered—hers or the meeting's, or both, we cannot tell; neither is it important to know. That soul believes in Jesus with exceeding joy. That is enough to know. But this is not all. Several other young persons—fourteen or fifteen in all—have sent in their requests for prayer from widely distant parts of the country, all saying they were in the same state of spiritual anxiety and distress on account of sin as the one who first wrote, and who soon after found peace in believing. They all desire prayer, that they too may find Christ.

CHAPTER XIV.

PERSONAL EFFORTS.

A tall man arose in one of the meetings and said:

"I am a clergyman, and my field of labor is in Key West, Florida—the most interesting field I have ever occupied, among a most interesting people. They are made up of sailors, soldiers, wreckers, ship-carpenters, longshoremen, fishermen, and almost all classes you can name, and of almost all nationalities. I preach to them several times every Sunday, and I pour the truth into willing ears and willing hearts. They are the most religious people I ever knew, and the most devoted Christians, so far as they are Christians at all.

"They must have family prayers three times a day —morning, noon, and night. They ask a blessing and return thanks at their meals; and if any little fellow gets away from the table during meal-time, he knows enough to get back before thanks are returned.

"I want to tell you how I built a church. There were a great number of spars, and masts, and ships' timbers scattered along the beach, belonging to nobody; they had been washed ashore from wrecks; so I thought out of these I would have a church. I told my plan to some of my people, and they approved of it. So I called the people together to help build.

"They came in great numbers, eager to help. When they gathered they said, 'Who is going to boss this job?' 'I am going to boss it myself,' I said; and so I off with coat, and they did the same, and went to work, and the way those spars and timbers flew into position was a caution. In thirty-two minutes by the watch after we commenced, we had a church built capable of holding and seating 1,000 people. I preached in that church every Sabbath afternoon at five o'clock, and the thousand seats are filled. Some have proposed to put a roof on it, but I wont have it. The sky is the sounding board of my pulpit, and I want nothing better.

"I speak very plainly to the ungodly among the people—terrible sermons—so that I am almost scared myself. I charge home upon them all that they are short of perfect righteousness through faith in the Lord Jesus Christ. I hold up to them what they are and what they ought to be, and with all the force I can I depict their certain and eternal ruin unless they repent. And my appeals are not in vain; many do turn to the Lord.

"Mine is the best church I ever saw in my life. They are the poorest and most ignorant I ever saw. They are called 'conchs,' 'crackers,' 'spongers,' 'fishers,' etc.; but they have the love of Jesus and the power of the Holy Spirit among them. Their life is hard, poor, and ignorant; but they accept a full gospel and a high standard of holy living. Their prayer-meetings are meetings of great power. A grand place to preach in is my five o'clock preaching church. It makes you feel as if you had full swing. Many hard characters have had legions of devils cast out of them. These men go out to do good as soon as they are born again. I tell them I would not give two bits for a Christian who would not try to make somebody else a Christian. I love these people, and I hope to live and die with them."

THE BRITISH PROVINCES.

A judge of the Court of the Queen's Bench, from one of the British Provinces, seized an early opportunity to address the meeting. He said:

"You do not know how much these meetings are doing in building up the kingdom of Christ. The reports of this meeting go far and wide. They are translated into other languages, and scattered among the nations of the earth. Many a Christian heart is cheered and roused to Christian action. I could tell you many incidents of good done through the influence of this meeting. I will give you only one. It was one night I was called to attend to a case of great distress. I found a man sunk down in deep despair by reason of intemperance. I found the poor inebriate a man of high education and culture, and his wife an educated and cultivated woman. I had read of the cases in this meeting, reformed and saved, in answer to prayer, for I read the redorts of this meeting every week. I took the man and his wife home to my house. I treated him as I would a brother, and now that man is a member of the same church with myself, and is a useful and happy Christian, and adorns his Christian profession by a well-ordered life. He is one of my class.

"I know of cases where our churches have asked you to pray for the outpouring of the Holy Spirit, and the showers of divine grace have come down in answer to prayer. I have the means of knowing something of the wide extent of your usefulness from an extensive correspondence. May God continue to pour upon this meeting the spirit of grace and supplication, and bless you in the future as He has done in the past. For ten years I have read the reports of this meeting, and in common with thousands on thousands I have been cheered and encouraged by them."

WITH POCKETS FULL.

Said one:

"I am going to the White Mountains, but I am not going to seek pleasure or rest. I am going with my pockets full of these," taking from his vest pockets some of the smallest sizes of the tracts published by the American Tract Society; "and by the distribution o' these and such as these I hope to do some good. I intend to make it my life work to win souls to the love and service of the Lord Jesus, and thus, while I minister to the health of my family, I hope to minister also to the spiritual wants of some souls ready to perish. Pray for me, and pray that these little things may be the means of salvation to many. In this humble way we may do good to dying men."

Then followed requests, not a few, for the continued outpouring of the Holy Spirit where revivals of religion are going forward in answer to prayer. One such comes from a prairie State, which says that the writer was once in this meeting, and he felt constrained to arise and call upon the meeting to pray for the outpouring of the Holy Spirit upon the place where he lived.

He went home and told the people what he had done, and those churches, with their pastors, agreed to give themselves to daily prayer, and though they are in a prairie country, and in the midst of hay and grain harvests, the people meet and hold day-time and night services every day, and a great number of leading and influential men have been converted.

A POOR IRISH BOY.

A missionary was visiting in his district in the city, and found a poor Irish boy once sick nigh unto death: indeed, he was in a dying state. He found the poor boy had been a member of a Sabbath-school, and he said to himself, "Oh! if I could only sing to him one of his Sabbath-school hymns." He could not think of anything so appropriate as the hymn—

>"Jesus, lover of my soul.
>Let me to thy bosom fly."

When he came to the stanza,

> "Other refuge have I none,
> Hangs my helpless soul on thee;
> Leave, oh, leave me not alone,
> Still support and comfort me,"

—the missionary noticed that the countenance of the dying boy lighted up with joy and gladness. So he asked him:

"What is your hope of salvation?"

The boy answered in a most touching manner:

"Other refuge have I none."

A fine-looking gentleman came up after the meeting and said to the leader:

"I am an Irishman, sir, and that little story of the poor Irish boy moved me exceedingly. I think the boy had found the true refuge. Oh! that we all could say from the heart, 'Other refuge have I none.'"

ANSWERS TO PRAYER.

A stranger said he wished to relate an incident that illustrates the power of prayer.

"A few years ago, a young lady was spending a few days at my house. She was a gay, fashionable young lady. One evening near the time of her leaving I spoke to her on the subject of religion. Her reply was, 'I do not want to be a Christian, and what is still more, I do not want you to talk to me on the subject.'

"But further conversation ensued. She remained at my house till a late hour. After musing for some time she at last said, very unexpectedly, 'Well, I suppose I might as well yield my heart to Christ to-night as any other time.'

"She did yield her heart to Christ, and since that eventful night she has proved herself a sincere and ardent Christian.

"Some time after this she visited us again, and said: 'Until yesterday I never knew why I was under such conviction of sin, and why I was led to give myself up to Jesus, so that that night became the night of my conversion. I have since learned that on that very day my brother had presented my case to the Boston Daily Noon Prayer Meeting, asking earnest prayer that I might at once be led out of darkness into God's marvellous light. Oh! it was all of God's grace, and in answer to prayer, that I was brought suddenly that night to turn to Jesus and consecrate myself to Him. I did not know then the secret of the mysterious power that moved me.'"

PERSONAL FAITHFULNESS.

One said:

"The Church needs almost more than anything else personal faithfulness in inviting sinners to come to Christ—faithfulness that shall seize opportunities to do good to everybody, under all circumstances and in every condition of life. Speaking to friends and neighbors and strangers, and endeavoring to bring them to repentance and faith in Christ, is the great thing wanted. You will find people far more willing to be spoken to in the proper manner than you suppose. There is a right way and there is a wrong way. You must seek to persuade sinners to lay hold on eternal life. You must be boiling over, so to speak, with love and sympathy for perishing souls. Then you will not speak in vain. You must go to them, not as constrained by duty, but you must go because you cannot help it."

Said a minister:

"I once had an elder in my church, who did not like the word resolution. He thought it savored of self too much. It speaks of what I am going to do if I can keep my resolution. I think I have a better word, and that word is consecration. Let a man be wholly consecrated to God, and he will do all duty in the right spirit and it will win; for the heart is in the work, and what a kind, loving heart does will win its way to the heart."

A young man appeared in the meeting, who said he came in behalf of a would-be suicide, from whom he had taken a pistol and a knife. The pistol he took from his pocket to give weight to his statements, which represented the man as on the verge of perdition. He asked prayer for his conversion, and continued:

"If he is saved, it will not be the first nor second suicide's life you have been the means of saving. Others, bent on self-destruction, you have snatched from the grave by your interposition. Pray for this poor man, who attempted suicide in the presence of his wife, and when he could not succeed with his pistol, then he undertook to use his knife. And his wife assisted in taking these murderous weapons from him."

Said another young man:

"It is prayer and personal effort. I knew a missionary in this city a year or two ago, who undertook to win 110 persons to Christ. He did this--wrote down the names of the 110. He prayed for each one, by name, every day. He visited one by one, as fast as he could, and prayed with them and endeavored to lead them to Christ. He continued this duty, and in one year, 100 of the 110 were converted. The facts are beyond all dispute."

This personal effort matter was alluded to by another speaker. He said it was this what first took hold of him, and continued:

"A young acquaintance came down to my office in Wall Street, and asked me if I would meet him at a certain hour for prayer together. I told him I would meet him. I have reason to thank God for that. It was the beginning of conviction, leading to conversion. I see that same young man here in the meeting. When I was converted, I did as he had done—invited another young man to a private place for prayer. He was converted. He is now here."

A sea captain, who had just returned, as he said, from a voyage, in which he had been very much blessed, said he could not let the meeting close without calling attention to one petition which the chairman had read at the opening of the meeting. It had affected him more than all the other petitions which had been read. It was an old one, perhaps, to some in the room, but it was new to him; at least it had been but a little time since he knew how to feel it. It ran in this way:

"'I beseech you therefore, brethren, by the mercies of God, that ye present your bodies, a living sacrifice, holy, acceptable unto God, which is your reasonable service.'

"That request takes all the wind out of my faith. I give all up. I must comply with it—body and soul —I give myself a living sacrifice to the Lord. No more my own, but all the Lord's."

YOUNG MEN AT WORK.

Said a speaker:

"I belong to a Young Men's Christian Association, and we resolved on a system of efforts to save souls. We went outside all means of grace, where the people lived in a state of semi-infidelity. They did not believe in God, man, or the devil—especially the last. It was in an English-speaking neighborhood that we secured a place to hold a prayer-meeting. It was in a private house that we held our first meeting, which was very hospitably and kindly offered us. We resolved to have no debate, no dispute about religion with the people. In the first place we would seek the presence and power of the Holy Spirit. We prayed to be baptized with power from on high. We were a little band of young men, all enlisted to do something in the Master's service. We began our work last November, holding meetings several times a week through the winter. We began by resolving to spend the time of our meetings in prayer and in the relation of our personal Christian experience, interspersed with devotional singing. We invited in all the neighbors around, and the first evening the room was full, and full of interest. We made our remarks short and our prayers short. If a man told what the Lord had done for his soul, he did it in as few, plain words as possible. The first meeting was a great success, and the goodly number present were deeply moved and themselves begged for another meeting. It was composed of non-worshippers and Sabbath-breakers in various forms. The householder, not knowing how otherwise to express his gratitude to them for holding the meeting in his house, asked them to drink with him a very choice glass of wine. They soon politely gave him to understand how they stood on the temperance question, and wine was not offered them a second time. We had crowded meetings. We had anxious ones in the meetings. We had in with us those who became convinced of the truths of our holy religion. We had those with us into whose mouths the Lord put a new song—even praise to His name. We have had all winter every now and then hopeful conversions. Our assemblage numbered thirty, forty, fifty, to as high as eighty persons at a gathering."

RUINED YOUNG MEN.

Any one coming into the meeting as a stranger would be surprised and pained at the great number of requests which come from mothers for prayers for intemperate, ruined sons. A mother begs for prayer as follows:

" Dear Christian Friends,—I notice so many answers to prayer for intemperate husbands and sons, that I ask, will you look once more to God on behalf of my only child and son, who, though much improved since I first asked your prayers, still seems powerless to resist temptation. Oh! do continue to pray that he may be cured of this appetite *now*, and for ever hate the cup; that he may resist temptation and look to Christ for help. Will you continue to pray for this dear one, till I can say the victory is gained, and thus help a poor mother in her prayers?"

A young man said:

" Yesterday I asked prayer for a young man who was anxious. He is my brother. This morning I called on him and asked him how he felt. 'This is the the way I feel,' he answered, handing me this leaflet from the American Tract Society."

The speaker held up the tract, and read the lines to which his brother pointed. It was entitled

COME.

"I have a Friend, a precious Friend,—unchanging, wise and true,
The chief among ten thousand, O! I wish you knew him too.
When all the woes that wait on me, relax each feeble limb,
I know who waits to welcome me—have you a Friend like Him?
He comforts me—He strengthens me; how can I then repine?
He loveth me. This faithful Friend in life and death is mine."

A WORD IN SEASON.

Said another:

"I was riding in a car, fifty miles from here, on a journey, and was seated by a lady, when we fell into conversation.

"She said, 'I know you sir.'

"'You know me? Where did you know me? I do not remember ever to have seen you before.'

"'Oh yes! I knew you at New Jersey, where you labored, and I have a daughter who will never forget you. She was one of the three hundred converted in the meetings there held, and she attributes her conversion to something that you said to her which was made the means of her awakening.'

"Another lady said she knew me, and she had a daughter, who would never forget me, converted at that meeting.

"I met a young man in the cars, a long distance from here. He came and shook me very warmly by the hand, and said he knew me.

"I said, 'I do not remember ever to have seen you.'

"'Oh yes! you have seen me, and this is what you

said to me: 'The great clock of eternity has no dialplate, and no hands. It is one eternal NOW. *Now* is the accepted time; behold, now is the day of salvation! Young man, this means your NOW—your opportunity. Come to Jesus *now*.' These words were made the means of my conversion, and I am now engaged in study for the ministry."

NO SOULS—SMALL SOULS.

A clergyman said that professedly infidel men not unfrequently profess to believe or disbelieve what they do not. He illustrated it by an occurrence in his own ministry. Years ago he resided at the West, and not far from his residence were living some pretty rough specimens of humanity, and yet they had many manly qualities about them. He sometimes went into neighborhoods to preach in their log school-houses, and he sometimes had the honor of preaching the Gospel to a singular class of human beings. Men would come into his meetings clothed in hunting shirts, as they were called, made of deer-skins, and trimmed very fancifully, bringing their rifles with them, and standing them up in a corner during the service. They were generally very orderly and attentive, and never attempted any disturbance. He continued:

"At one time I had been preaching in a log school-house on the value of the soul, from Christ's own words, wherein He says: 'What shall it profit a man if he gain the whole world and lose his own soul, or what shall a man give in exchange for his soul?' I had preached as solemn and earnest a sermon as possible.

"I rode away from the place of preaching on horseback, and presently a man came to my side, also on horseback, and we proceeded along the road together. He was a burly-looking, strong man, of good appearance and good manners, and evidently on the best of terms with himself, as thinking that he knew something. He was disposed to conversation, and called up the sermon.

"'Stranger,' said he, 'that was a pretty good sermon of yours, only there was not a word of truth in it.'

"'What part of it do you object to?' said I, somewhat surprised.

"'I mean no offence, sir,' said he, bowing, 'but I do not believe in souls!'

"'Do you mean to say that we have no souls?'

"'Exactly so, sir; no soul at all.' And passing his hand along down the neck of the fine horse he was riding, he added, 'I do not believe I have any more soul than this horse has,' and he looked up with a look of self-satisfaction.

"I replied, 'Sir'—speaking with all due solemnity, while I felt the twinkles that must have been around my eyes—'I have met with men having very small souls indeed'—emphasizing 'small'—'but I must confess that I have never met a man before who had no soul at all.'

"He was in a towering passion in a moment, and looking at me with a look which he supposed would wither me, said: 'I'll have you to know, sir, that I have just as large a soul as anybody.'

"I assured him I meant no offence. I was only taking him on his own ground—that he had no soul, which I insisted must be an error, as he evinced that he had soul enough to resent what he took for an insult. We rode on several miles together, entering into and keeping up a pleasant conference, in which I attempted to prove to him the existence and immortality of the soul, and set forth the vast forever on which it must soon enter. I fancied I made some impression. At any rate I made him my friend, and had afterward the satisfaction of admitting him and his wife into the church to which I ministered.

"In my first interview with him, I succeeded in convincing him that he did not believe his own assertions, and no reasonable man could. We have souls to be saved or lost, and every man knows that he is bound on an unending voyage of happiness or woe. Men may cavil, but they cannot deny. They cannot cut the cords which bind them to the eternal future, and they know it."

CHAPTER XV.

THE CONVERT'S HOUR.

The meeting was led by a young man, who read a short portion of Scripture, which brought up the matter for immediate decision, whether we would be on the Lord's side or not—" Choose ye this day whom ye will serve." In a few remarks he urged the importance of deciding the great question *now*, in this accepted time, and *now*, in this day of salvation. He said he insisted on it, because *now* is all the time we have. It is not to-morrow nor yesterday—it is now. It is our only moment—all there is of life is in the instant present.

He said a young lady came into one of their prayer-meetings in Brooklyn, where a deep religious interest was prevailing. She came out of a wealthy, worldly family, thoughtless on this whole subject. She became impressed that her whole eternity hung upon her decision in that meeting; and though she came in with the great question of her eternal well-being unsettled, she resolved to have it all settled then and there, and before the hour of prayer had passed away, and to be on the Lord's side forever more. He said he knew there were young men in the room who had never decided this all-important question, and he hoped they would not delay a moment. Then he read a large number of requests for prayer.

One was from a widow, whose only son in early life made a profession of religion, but, judging from his subsequent life, she feared he was deceived. She said: "Pray earnestly that God will now grant him true and unfeigned repentance and faith in the Lord Jesus Christ, that he may, by a life of prayer and good works, glorify his Father who is in heaven." She added: "Your prayers have been answered in the conversion of four of his associates. God is waiting and willing to be gracious. Pray in faith."

Let us come boldly to the throne of grace. There's no prayer without faith. Confidence in God, as faithful to all His promises, must be the cause and the encouragement of all true prayer. We must believe God to be as good as His word, and that He is the rewarder of those who diligently seek Him. The process by which we gain this confidence in God we now can explain. We cannot reason above it. It is the gift of God. How God gives it we cannot tell, or why He gives it at one time and not at another we cannot answer.

Though faith is the gift of God, we believe it is not given without asking and seeking for it. And we believe no gift is so freely bestowed as the gift of faith when we really desire it. So, if we are faithless and unbelieving, we are utterly without excuse. Faith is heroic and joyful in God when it is in lively exercise. Faith on wings of prayer is a mighty power. We cannot measure it.

A large number were before the authorities of the church for examination for church-membership. They wished to make public profession of their faith in Christ. Among the number was the wife of a captain of a vessel plying between New York and Philadelphia. On the evening of the very Sabbath day on which this faithful, devoted wife united herself with the church by a public profession of her faith in Christ, that husband was in his cabin, alone, in the harbor of New York, and on the next Sabbath evening he was in a prayer-meeting, in Philadelphia, to tell what had been his religious experience for one week. Now hear what that experience was, and mark how God answers prayer, as appears in the religious history of one week. This captain gave substantially the following account of himself:

"I was alone in my cabin in the port of New York on the evening of the day on which my wife, unknown to myself, united herself with the church. All at once there came over my mind a strange solemnity. I wondered what made me feel so. I did not know what it was. I felt restless under it and endeavored to shake it off. I took up some light reading which I had with me in the cabin, and thought that by bestowing my attention upon that I might be able to create a diversion of feeling and turn it into another channel or drive it away. But it was of no use, I tried and tried to banish that solemnity, and the more I tried the more it clung to me. Seeing a New Testament lying upon the table, I took it and opened it at the 15th chapter of the Gospel according to John. I read it through very attentively, it made a deep impression upon my heart, I thought what wonderful language it was, what a wonderful character it revealed. I wished I could be among those to whom those gracious words were addressed. I felt how great a sinner I was, and how much I needed a Saviour to interpose in my behalf and save me. I went to my state-room and turned the key in the lock, and knelt down and endeavored to pray. I prayed for mercy and forgiveness. I implored, with deep penitence for my sins, a free and full pardon, and it came. I did not leave that state-room that night till I had peace with God through our Lord Jesus Christ."

At the prayer-meeting this captain said that at the very hour when he was awakened, and felt an invisible hand laid upon him, his praying wife was pleading with God for his salvation. He said he was there to join his wife in profession of attachment to Christ, and publicly espouse his cause. "And now," continued the speaker, "you see the fulfilment of the promise that 'before they call I will answer, and while they are yet speaking I will hear.'" Here was a careless, prayerless man, without any influence but a Divine influence, arrested while alone in the cabin of his ship in a distant port, and brought immediately to repentance and faith in Christ. All things are possible with God. Only believe that ye receive the things ye ask and ye shall have them. Faith on the wings of prayer had carried this sea captain to a throne of grace. That new-born Christian, his devoted, praying wife had power with God.

One said:

"I can keep silent no longer. I have never before spoken a word in a religious meeting. I have been coming here for three weeks past, in a state of great religious anxiety. I believe I have very lately been made the happy subject of God's renewing grace. I feel assured that all my sins, for Christ's sake, have been pardoned and blotted out forever. I give myself to Jesus, to confess, and honor, and love, and obey him before men. I make this public confession of my faith in Him. I enter upon a new life, and this is my deliberate act and choice; and I feel that I am moved to it by the Holy Spirit. I am exceedingly happy in it. I love this holy place of prayer. I love those who meet here to pray. I beg young men, here in this meeting, distressed about their sins as I was, to come at once and lay all their burdens down at the foot of the cross."

When he had closed, another arose and said he had strayed in with no particular purpose in view; but he had not come in a second time without feeling that he was a great sinner, and he came hoping he might find Christ here, and he believed he had found Him. He could say—

"I lay my sins on Jesus,
The spotless Lamb of God."

"I have great peace in believing in Him. I exhort my fellow young men in this room to make trial of Jesus' love to-day."

Another arose and poured forth the praise of a full heart for what Jesus had done for him. His language was very beautiful, and even poetical, without his seeming to know it. His great desire seemed to be to express the joy and surprise he felt in the assurance that Jesus had spoken peace to his troubled spirit—so that where there was a great whirlwind of conflicting emotions, there was now a great calm. His appeals to the unconverted were very touching.

Another young man proceeded to say, with great emotion:

"I never was in the Fulton Street Prayer Meeting but once before, and that was when you met in the old church. I entered the church a perfect stranger, not a soul knowing me, or I them. I sat down in a corner. I had read of the meeting, and that the Spirit of God was there. I had not been long in the meeting, not many minutes, before I felt He was there, for I felt His power moving my heart to believe in Jesus. I had come into the meeting in great pecuniary trouble, not knowing what to do. I made up my mind, then and there, that the first thing was to make sure of Christ for a friend, and take Him into my heart as a Saviour. Then I resolved to ask and expect Him to help me from that time forth, forever and ever, according to my needs and wants. I found peace from that moment. I resolved to leave at once for the West, where I believed business would open for me. I went, according to my resolution, and was greatly prospered. I am on my journey eastward. Passing through the city, I felt it my duty to come in here and say to you how dear to my heart is this Fulton Street Prayer Meeting. This was truly to my soul the house of God and the gate of heaven. God be praised that I ever heard of it, ever read of it, for He has made it the means of salvation to my soul. I bear my humble testimony for Christ wherever I go. I can truly say—

"'Jesus, I my cross have taken,
All to leave and follow Thee.'"

A WELCOME LETTER.

The following letter was read to the meeting, which caused fervent thanksgiving:

"To the Friends of the Fulton Street Prayer Meeting: Some time ago I sent a request to your meeting for prayer for myself, a poor, wicked young girl. It did seem to me there was no mercy for me, I was so wicked.

"For some time I had desired to ask your prayers, but dared not. At last, as I told you, I read how so many found peace. I determined to try once more to seek the salvation of my soul. And when I read the answer to my request in the paper, and of the prayer that was offered and the remarks of the leader of the meeting, I wept tears of thankfulness. Those words touched my hardened heart, and I fell on my knees and asked God to have mercy on me. And He did. I now feel that your prayers have been answered, and to-day I am rejoicing in the precious blood of Christ, my glorious Redeemer. Although I am weak, He can make me strong. Oh, how I should love to clasp every one of you by the hand, for I love you all as God's dear children.

"I shall ever pray for the Fulton Street Prayer Meeting."

A young man said:

"Three weeks ago to-day, I trust, I was led to know the way of salvation. I had struggled for this experimental knowledge I meant to conquer—a peace with God by my own efforts, until I was led to despair of help within myself, and to turn to that Power that is mighty to save. And as soon as I did that I felt that I was saved, with an everlasting salvation. I cannot tell you how happy I have been.

Another young man gave a similar account of his

wonderful experience of a Saviour's pardoning love. He had found salvation in this very room, by believing in Jesus Christ.

FIVE SONS CONVERTED.

One day a great many mothers sent in for prayer for their impenitent sons, and more than one had asked the meeting to offer thanksgiving for their conversion. One wrote:

"This is my third request. In the first I asked you to pray for the conversion of my five sons. In answer to prayer, as I verily believe, three of my dear boys were hopefully converted. I wrote again for joyful thanksgiving to be offered, and for continued prayer. Now I write to tell you that the remaining two have been called into the kingdom of Christ by the effectual calling of the Holy Spirit. Oh, this is wonderful grace! I cannot tell you what a mother feels under such a gracious hand as this. I feel humbled in the dust under a sense of my unworthiness of so much mercy. Will you not offer thanksgivings with me when you read this to the meeting, and pray that God will incline my sons to recommend Christ to sinners while they live, and make them the means of winning many to him?"

Many a mother's heart will be moved as she reads the story of these conversions, and may be encouraged to pray and believe that her own sons will be converted. Who can tell where the influence of these conversions will end—five sons converted? "Yes," said the leader; "yes we will offer thanksgivings to the God of all grace for these answers to prayer, and for every example of the Spirit's gracious power."

A young man arose and said:

"Some of you will remember me. I am one of those sons converted in this meeting in answer to the prayers of praying mothers. I had a praying mother, whose pleadings at the throne of grace were answered. I was, as I trust, converted in this room, to which I was invited to come. Here Jesus was revealed to me as a Prince and a Saviour as never before. Oh, how lovely and loving did He appear! This was eight months ago. I came every day for some time. I was filled with a longing desire to preach the Gospel. But I was without means of preparation. I did not know how to get them. At length I concluded if the Lord wanted me to preach the Gospel, He would provide the means of preparation. One evening, a gentleman sent me word he wished to see me. He was a stranger. I went to his house, and he received me with great cordiality, and wished me to tell him my religious experience, and how I came to be anxious about my soul. I began with my dear praying mother, and ended with what God had done for me in this prayer-meeting. He seemed to be deeply affected. After hearing my story, he said: 'I understand you wish to study for the ministry. I shall be happy to give you all the means you require.' I have now been at the seminary several months, and I have the prospect of continued support."

A LETTER FROM A YOUNG CONVERT.

"It is but lately that I have found my Saviour. A short time ago a request was sent from this church for an interest in your prayers. They have been answered already; for, on the last Sabbath there were thirty-five added to the church on profession of their faith. I make this earnest request for three young men, hoping and praying that our united prayers may be speedily answered."

A Western man said:

"Two years ago, I was in a bank in Illinois. The cashier said to me: 'When you get to New York, go to the Fulton Street Prayer Meeting, and tell them that a boy residing three miles from here was a very hard case. I finally concluded to send a request to you to make him a subject of prayer. He has recently been hopefully converted, and I wish the brethren in New York to know it.'"

WRONG AGAIN.

A young lady came into the meeting late, and took a seat near the pulpit. She requested one sitting by her to ask the meeting to pray for one "anxious to become a Christian to-day." The case was stated. A clergyman was conducting the exercises. He said they would sing one verse:

"' Just as I am, without one plea
But that Thy blood was shed for me,
And that Thou bidd'st me come to Thee,
O Lamb of God! I come.'"

The singing concluded, instantly a poor newsboy was on his feet, with the earnest simplicity of a child, and in well-chosen language was pouring out his heart to God for the immediate conversion of this young lady. We have rarely heard a more appropriate prayer. It was completely divested of the ordinary forms of expression, but all felt how near it came to the mercy-seat. It was the earnest pleading of a heart with God for the salvation of this anxious young lady—"to-day, on the spot, now in this very room." The meeting seemed to be in hearty sympathy with this prayer, and the subject of it. Prayer after prayer followed.

As soon as the meeting had received the benediction, the minister made his way to this anxious young lady, who stood in a slip near the pulpit. We stood near enough to hear the conversation. She stood with a smile on her face, and her eyes at times full of tears. It was the old story—a blind heart, anxious for the great change, but she could not see how to procure it.

He dealt with her kindly and faithfully, and preached to her "Jesus, the Way, the Truth, and the Life;" told her salvation was by faith in Christ. She must believe in Him. She told him she knew it all, but she could not believe; she could not make herself believe; she wished she could. He saw she was trying to do something for herself, to work out a righteousness of her own. She had not seen herself in that light; she knew that was wrong. "What must I do, then? It seems as if I must do something," she said. "Yes, you must do something. There is only one thing you can do: Believe on the Lord Jesus Christ."

"And be a Christian with no more feeling than I have got now? I supposed there would be a great change."

"So there will be when your heart really consents to believe in Jesus. As to feeling less or more, as one of the terms of salvation, the Gospel does not say a word about that—makes no requirements."

She stood looking uncertain and bewildered. She seemed to have all that swept away which she had imagined as a process through which she was to pass before she reached the great change; and she was shut up to just that one thing—BELIEVING. She saw it, and that strange smile deepened as she said: "I will try."

"Oh! no! no!" she was answered; "don't say you will try. Here is the old self-righteousness again coming in that little sentence: 'I will try.' Don't say that. Rather say: 'Lord, I believe! Help Thou mine unbelief!'"

The minister said he must go, and bade her good-bye. She hastened to say: "Will you pray for me!"

"Oh! no! no! wrong again! depending on my prayers, on the prayers of this meeting, or on the prayers of your Christian friends. Don't depend on these. Depend on Jesus, just Him, and on nothing and nobody else. Of course, I shall pray for you," and he was gone. She was there again the next day, with feelings changed somewhat, apparently "not far from the kingdom of heaven," if she was not already in it.

NO CHURCH GOOD ENOUGH.

A request was read asking prayer for two young men, who gave as their excuse for not attending to the claims of religion that, on looking around, they could find no church good enough for them to join; no church good enough for them to have any confidence in their prayers; no church whose example they would like to follow. "Why," said they, " if we could not live more consistent lives than these people, we would not make any pretensions to religion." But, in the merciful providence of God, both these young men were awakened to a sense of their sins and became converted, and joined the very church whose members they had so much derided.

Said the speaker:

"One day, I met these young men, and reminding

them of what they had said, asked them how they were getting along. 'Oh, don't ask me?' said one; 'don't say anything about it. It seems as if the very devil was let loose to torment us the moment we entered upon a religious life. It is temptation here, and temptation there, and temptation everywhere; and the more godly we try to live, the more ungodly we seem to ourselves to be. We have hard work to beat Satan back, and keep him from getting the mastery over us. Without Jesus we could not stand a moment.'

"'Then you do not think you are so much better than all the church now?'

"'No, indeed; we are the least of all, and are not worthy to be numbered with the people of God at all.'

"'Then it is not so very easy work to live a better life than others,' I said.

"'Oh, don't talk—don't talk; we make bad work enough of it. It is not what we thought it was at all. It is a constant fight with foes within and foes without. And yet we are kept by the power of God unto salvation, through faith in Christ Jesus.'

"I see these young men often. They, I have no doubt, are fighting the good fight of faith, and are thus laying hold of eternal life. But they have their troubles and trials, like all other Christians. They are well cured of their contempt of ordinary Christians, because they are no better."

A YOUNG MAN CONVERTED.

A young man arose and said that for about ten

days he had been coming steadily to these meetings. He had been awakened at these meetings. He had been converted, as he hoped. It had been all the work of the Holy Spirit. He had been alone. And now he must tell what a change had come over all his views, and feelings, and prospects. So here he stood, a monument of God's mercy. It was all the work of the Spirit of God.

He said that, after the change in his own heart, he felt as if he ought to converse with his room-mate, boarding with him at the same hotel. He knew he was a Roman Catholic. But he knew nothing more of his religious opinions. He also knew that he was about leaving for France. He thought he could not let him depart till he had told him of the change in himself, and had recommended to him the same Saviour he had found. So he opened up all his mind to him. He told him of the change in himself. He was surprised to hear that room-mate say that he was in the same anxious condition in which he had been. He was going on board ship, and off for France, and for home, with a moral necessity upon him which deprived him of all happiness. It was indeed a case of conviction of sin, and need of a Saviour, which lay like a heavy burden upon his soul.

A man arose in the back part of the room. He

was a man in middle life, and apparently of more than ordinary intelligence. He said:

"I have been coming here for some time. For a few days I have felt that I was born again—begotten anew in Christ Jesus. Some who hear me will be astonished to hear me say it. They know that I have been proud in saying that I would not believe what I could not understand. But I am free to say I cannot understand how God could have mercy on a wretch like me. But wretch as I was, Jesus has spoken peace to me. It was surprising grace. I want to say to all anxious ones here and everywhere, make but trial of His grace and love, and see how precious He is. O, so precious."

CANNOT TELL.

A letter was read from one awakened by simply reading an account of how God hears and answers prayer in this meeting, and she, the writer, was encouraged to hope the same might be true in regard to her. Whose prayers were answered—hers or the meeting's, or both, we cannot tell; neither is it important to know. That soul believes in Jesus with exceeding joy. That is enough to know. But this is not all. Several other young persons—fourteen or fifteen in all—sent in their requests for prayer from widely distant parts of the country—all saying they were in the same state of spiritual anxiety and distress on account of sin, as the one who first wrote, and who soon after found peace in believing. They all desire prayer, that they too may find Christ. The case was stated as above to the meeting. Some of these had said that they did not understand how to believe in Christ. They knew it must be done, but they did not see how to take the first step.

A gentleman arose and said:

"It is no wonder these do not understand how to believe in Christ. No man understands it. He cannot tell how he believes, if he does believe. All he can say is, 'Whereas I was blind now I see.' He cannot tell how the step was taken from a state of unbelief to a state of faith in Jesus. No man, no angel in heaven, can tell how the step is taken from condemnation to justification. All we know is that it is taken A man may undertake to reason about it. But he can not. He cannot philosophize about it. Faith is the gift of God. It is above reason. It is a new creation in the soul. A man believes in Jesus. He cannot tell how it came about. He cannot explain. It is above explanation. 'With the heart man believeth unto righteousness.' No man can say how he does it. The man has been made 'a new creature in Christ Jesus.' Old things have passed away. All things have become new. All these," he continued, "have made the common mistake. They think they must do something, and they are determined to do it. They are going to help on the great change. They are going to do in this just as they have done in the things of the world. They have always thought that they must get hold of the great crank which governed motion and make things move. And God lets men try till they find they have done and can do nothing. The Lord means to let us understand how helpless we are. The whole matter of faith aims to two points. It is letting go—and it is taking hold. It is letting go of sin, and it is taking hold on Jesus as a Saviour. It is letting go of things below, and it is taking hold on things above. It is letting go of our own righteousness, and it is taking hold of the righteousness of God. The heart really does this, and yet no man can tell how it does it. We cannot school ourselves into it. We cannot say, 'I will believe in Jesus,' times enough, over and over, in a lifetime, to make ourselves believe in Him. We must go to God for this faith. We must ask Him to give it to us, and it must be the mighty cry of the heart in our helplessness and hopelessness, crying, 'Lord, save, or I perish.' Man's extremity is God's opportunity."

CHAPTER XVI.

ONE IN CHRIST JESUS.

THE meeting on this occasion was led by a veteran Sunday-school teacher, who was formerly a member of Rev. Dr. Milner's church, St. George's, in Beekman Street. He read the 17th chapter of John, and commented on it very briefly, and gave some points in his own religious experience in connection with it. He said he well remembered the night, in a room not very far from this place of prayer, when his whole soul was in an awful state of opposition to God, and, if it had been possible, he would have hurled Him from His throne. No language could describe the struggle that prevailed in his bosom between his own will and the will of God. The Holy Spirit strove with him, and he strove against the Holy Spirit. But in the morning the contest was ended, and it has never been renewed. It was a submission to the will of God that was full of joy and peace. The old man was laid low, and the new man was exalted. He said he was born a second time, into the spirit of this 17th chapter of John, and he could never cease to feel the bond which binds all

Christian hearts together. It was Christ's prayer that we should be one. It is Christ's work that makes us one. Who are we that Jesus has purchased with his own precious blood, that we should not be what he prayed for in this prayer—one in Christ Jesus.

A stranger arose and said he had heard and read of this meeting, but had never been in it before. He was from a long way off, and he was going a long way off over the mighty deep. He had been in the habit, for years, of uniting with this meeting in prayer when twelve o'clock came. He knew others who did the same. He said he was on his way to his dear native land, Ireland, and he should tell them of this meeting. He was not ignorant of its prosperity. He was engaged in the same work, and wherever he went he tried to win souls to Christ. His pockets he said were full of tracts, and his mouth of arguments; and as God gave him opportunities, he prayed for grace and heart to improve them.

In another moment a minister arose and expatiated briefly upon the prayer of the blessed Saviour, that his people might be one. This is the great end of love to God and love to man. The whole church is moving towards the unity of the Spirit. We must be one in a stronger sense than can be shadowed forth by any visible ties.

There next came a request from a pastor that we will pray for the Holy Spirit to be poured out upon a church which commences a meeting in Tennessee. They read of answers to prayer and they feel assured that they shall have a great blessing. "And they will," said the leader, as he read the request, "if they do not have faith in us, but have faith in God. We ought to pray, and so should they, and at the same time say, 'The power belongeth unto God.' Let us remember this church in Tennessee."

On the first day of the fifteenth year of prayer there came in fifty-two requests for supplication, for almost all classes of persons and from widely remote places. The most touching of them all, perhaps, was the following one from the other side of the globe, sent by a native church in India, under the care of the American Board, written in the language of that country, and translated by the resident missionary, who writes as follows:

AHMEDNUGGER, INDIA.
August 12, 1871.

"*To the Fulton Street Prayer Meeting.*

"DEAR BRETHREN: The enclosed letter is from a native church in this place, and will explain itself. At our monthly concert, on the 7th inst, I read from home papers, translating some accounts of your meetings, which, as they always do, awakened much interest. Before the meeting closed, it was voted to send this request. Our annual meeting comes in October, the month in which this request will probably come before you. I join my request with that of the church. Brethren, pray for us, especially that we may have the Spirit's reviving influence at that time. Below is a translation of Pastor Modak's letter.

"Your missionary brother, L. BISSEL."

The letter of this native pastor was a curiosity, being written in Hindostanee, apparently with great care. It is as follows:

"*To the Fulton Street Prayer Meeting, New York, America:*

"We, the native Christian Church of Ahmednuggur, India, in connection with the Mahratta mission of the American Board, send an earnest request that you will pray for us, that we may all, both great and small, be filled with the Holy Spirit, and that many of the careless multitude around us may be turned to Christ. We learn from accounts of your meetings that you have constant communication with our heavenly Father. Though you are far from us, even by the telegraphic routes, yet by the telegraphic line of prayer we are near, so that when your prayers for us shall reach the mercy-seat of our heavenly Father, there will be no delay or other hindrance to our receiving the blessing. Be pleased, then, to accept this, our request. This letter is sent by the unanimous consent of all the members of our church.

"Signed, your brother in Christ,

"R. V. MODAK."

This letter being read, a clergyman was on his feet in a moment, offering up most fervent supplications that this little band of Christians in that far-off land might be like a well-watered garden of the Lord— watered by the showers of heavenly grace. An elder of the same church sent several requests for prayer for various objects. He had been a Mohammedan, and he asks us to pray for his Mohammedan teacher, also for his brother, who is of the same religious belief, also for the church, the pastor, his wife and "good children," and himself, that God will pour out His Spirit upon them all, and bring the spiritually dead to life, and a life of repentance and faith in Christ. It was said in the meeting to-day: "As we enter on this fifteenth year of prayer, we should bring the churches here to be prayed for, and we should ask them to pray for us." One man said: "We are on the eve of great events—just as it was in 1857, when the whole land received such a spiritual refreshing."

About the time of the fourteenth anniversary of the Fulton Street Prayer Meeting there came a request for prayer from India, sent by a church of native Christians, written in Hindostanee, accompanied by a translation made by an American missionary. It came into the meeting while the anniversary exercises were going on. Dr. Hall, the reader, read it to the meeting, and remarked that he should call upon one who had been upon heathen ground to respond to that request, and he called upon a Wesleyan missionary to lead in prayer. It was an earnest supplication offered to Jesus—pleading His promise, "Lo! I am with you alway."

Now, mark what follows, as narrated in a letter. The following has just been received from the same church:

"Ahmednugger, India,
November 10, 1871.
"*To the Fulton Street Prayer Meeting:*

"Dear Brethren: Some months since we sent you a request to pray for us, that we might be revived, and increased in spiritual strength. From the New York *Evangelist* of September 28th, we learn that our request came before you at your annual meeting, and that we were earnestly remembered at the throne of grace. We write this to thank you, and tell you briefly how your prayers were answered. A daily prayer-meeting was commenced by the church on the first day of October, and continued till the time of our annual meeting in the last week of the month. In that time we were favored in having with us Rev. W. Taylor, the evangelist, and God blessed his labors among us, so that we continued our special efforts for two weeks—holding two services daily. Many of the Christians were revived, confessed their sins, and gave themselves anew unto the Lord. Some who had been long listening to the word came forward and professed their faith in Christ, and were received into the church. The heathen, who seldom attend our preaching, came in crowds, and some, we trust, received lasting impressions for good. For all these spiritual blessings bestowed in answer to your and our united prayers, we ask you to join with us in thanksgiving to God. And again remember us, and the labors of the Rev. Mr. Taylor, who is holding a series of meetings in Bombay. O that God would rend the heavens and come down, and cause that the mountains of idolatry and caste might flow down at His presence, and that Hindostan might be given to the Lord Jesus Christ! Amen.

"In behalf of the church,
"V. MODAK, Pastor."

A minister arose and said:

"I have recently come from attending a meeting of the Friends at Glenn's Falls. I went there to see and hear how much of Christ I should hear and see exhibited there in that meeting, and I am happy to tell you that nowhere has Jesus—crucified and slain for our offences, and risen again for our justification—been more fully preached than in that meeting. And the consequence has been that the Spirit has come down in great power, and great numbers have become obedient to the faith as it is in Jesus. The movement was much as it was in Brooklyn, and I regard this revival Spirit among the Friends as one of the wonders of the age. It is clearly in line with that great movement of the age which manifests the union of all believers in Jesus—'fulfilling his prayer one in me.' Oh! how slow the church has been to manifest this oneness, this unity of the Spirit. But God is bringing it about, and this revival among the Friends is of no human power. No human means could bring it about. It is all of God. I saw men and women, old men and maidens bowed down under a sense of their sins, and I saw them, in great numbers, full of joy as having found Christ by the exercise of faith in Him. The revival had all the features of a genuine work of grace. It was still and powerful. Great was the company of believers."

As soon as opportunity was given, a minister of the German Reformed church arose, said a few words in regard to the oneness of spirit which was gaining ground in all branches of the Christian church. Said he:

"The hour is come. What hour? The hour when the world shall know that there is one church of God on earth—when denominational names are lost sight of—when there shall be one dominion and Jesus Christ shall be King of kings and Lord of lords."

He was followed by an Episcopal minister, who said it had been some time since he had been in this meeting. He never felt the oneness of the church so much anywhere else as here; and *here*, because it is elsewhere and coming to be everywhere. We are one with Christ, and we are one among ourselves.

A Presbyterian minister said:

"Yes, and this oneness must have a visible manifestation. Christ said the world must know and feel it. It is said to be a spiritual oneness. What does the world know about a spiritual oneness? They know nothing about that. They only know so far as they see. They must have something to see."

A man arose and said:

"I want you to let me say one word. I am from a long way off, and I am going a long way off across the great deep. But I have for years read of this meeting. I have often said if I can ever get to New York I will find the Fulton Street Prayer Meeting. Thank God I am here! I felt a holy influence on me as soon as I entered the door. I know God's Holy Spirit abides here. We all feel His presence and His power. I have read the books which have been written about the answers to prayer—wonderful they are. I shall tell them in Ireland, my own native land, that I have been here; and another thing I will tell you, that for a long, long time I have observed this hour of prayer, I have prayed with you. I know others who do the same. We pray for every burdened soul who comes here for prayer. Oh! down, down with our church distinctions. Let Christ alone be exalted. Let us give our hands to one another and our hearts to Jesus, and have the song in our mouths—

'Blest be the tie that binds
Our hearts in Christian love.'"

The meeting arose and sang the whole hymn, and

then the benediction was pronounced by a voice that trembled with the deep emotion of the hour and the occasion.

"The grace of our Lord Jesus Christ, and the love of God, and the communion of the Holy Ghost be with you all, Amen."

Some time ago, a merchant of one of the Southern States, when in New York, visited the Fulton Street Prayer Meeting, accompanied by several members of his family. He had several times previously visited that sacred place of prayer and felt the power of the divine presence. He had also sent many requests for prayer, in behalf of friends near and dear, to the meeting, and on the occasion referred to, before the commencement of the meeting, he hastily put on paper a few sentences and sent them to the leader of the meeting, asking that thanks be given to the hearer and answerer of prayer for blessed answers to their united requests.

Unaccustomed to public speaking, and with a heart too full for utterance, he did not trust himself to appear before the meeting. To his surprise after the leader had read the few lines he had written, he called upon the brother from South Carolina to lead in prayer, if in the room. The Spirit whispered, Stand up for Jesus, and with aspirations to heaven for help, the brother arose and gave a narrative of events and experiences of divine mercy. He found his feelings were overcoming him and he begged that some brother would offer thanksgiving in his stead. A venerable Christian man near him arose and poured out such a heart full of thanksgivings that many of the audience were melted to tears.

After the meeting one and another of the brethren present extended to him hearty greetings, and he soon found, though among earthly strangers, the expressions of love betokened that he was among dearest friends.

Going to his hotel, he sat down and immediately wrote to the remainder of his family at home of the blessings he had enjoyed in the Fulton Street Prayer Meeting. The letter reached its destination on a day in the evening of which there was a social prayer-meeting at the house of a friend. The letter was handed to the pastor, who read it to the meeting. In the meeting was a minister who had a little charge some miles away. His congregation was apparently cold and dead, and this minister prayed fervently that God would revive his work greatly among his own people. Riding home the next day his mind was busy, and he determined to make use of what he had heard the previous evening. He related it to several of the young men, and they determined to hold a prayer-meeting in the church. Meantime the merchant returned home, and meeting this minister gave him one of the large hand-bills of the Fulton Street meeting, and he nailed it on the door of the church, where it attracted much attention. The appointment for the village prayer-meeting was duly published: It was something unusual, and was the subject of favorable and unfavorable comment. When the hour came the pastor took his place as the leader, who poured out his heart to God that He would open a window in heaven and shower down the rain of the heavenly grace upon them. Toward the close of the meeting he asked if there was any one present who desired to speak with him more privately, or to be prayed for. If so, he would meet any such in the school-house near at hand. The pastor entered alone and lighted a candle, and sat some time in solitude. Presently a young man entered, and without a word sank down upon his knees, soon another and another came and took the same attitude, and the whole group joined in prayer. Some time was thus spent, when they dispersed. There was little sleep for pastor or people that night. The minister had scarcely closed his eyes when a loud knocking was heard. He arose and went to the door in the dark, when suddenly a pair of arms were around his neck and the first young man who entered the school-house had come to tell him that he had found Jesus. The glorious work spread from one to another. In some places those who ridiculed the prayer-meetings one day would be found to be in agony on account of their sins the next, and be pleading for mercy. In a little time twenty-six were ready to be baptized and admitted to the church. One inquired of the merchant:

"Do you know where this work of grace began?"

"Where do you suppose it began?" inquired the merchant.

"It began with your visit to the Fulton Street Prayer Meeting."

This narrative of a few facts shows that we cannot measure the good which may be accomplished by one little prayer-meeting, begun and conducted in the right spirit. It also shows how willing God is to hear and answer prayer, and it shows, too, how ready we should be to pray. A little spark often kindles a great fire.

CHAPTER XVII.

PARENTS AND CHILDREN.

A young man gave account of his own conversion. He said he had a praying mother, and she became very anxious that he should go with her to the prayer-meeting, but he refused to go—appealing to his father to know what he had better do about it. His father told him that if he did not want to go to the prayer-meeting he had better stay at home; and advised his mother to stay at home with him. She did stay, but she stayed to pray. She took him away with her into a room alone, and all the heart of a pious mother was moved within her on that occasion. Said he:

"She prayed as if she thought I was sinking into perdition. Such was her earnestness that it touched my heart, and I felt as if I was lost. I was in great distress of mind—saw myself a ruined sinner, and found no rest till I found it in believing in Jesus."

The young man spoke in a very fervid manner, and no written words can convey an idea of the impression produced. It was much as many other things which transpire in these meetings: they cannot be described. The young speaker continued:

"I am not willing to take my seat till I have made one appeal to the young men here and urged them to come to Christ. I have never been happy till now, and never knew what happiness was."

Another spoke of a scene of a very different character. He had been South after the remains of a young man who had been accidentally shot. A short time ago he was converted at the Greenwich Street Prayer Meeting. Before his conversion he was a fast young man—an only son—living at one of our fashionable hotels—spending his father's substance in riotous living—a prodigal. But God met him in His mercy. He joined a church up-town—sat down once at the communion-table—went South to reside for some years—was suddenly called away. His religion went with him to the South. There he sought the society of the pious—there he comforted the poor—there he endeavored to lead sinners to Christ. He left these blessed evidences behind him that the good work which had been wrought within him was of God. Happy tokens of the "great change." His remains were brought on North by the gentleman who was addressing us. He called upon the meeting in behalf of the father, then present with him, to render thanks to God for the conversion of this young man. Now he sleeps in the very spot where he had said to his father he should like to be buried, before he parted with him for the last time.

NEVER GIVE UP TRUSTING IN GOD.

Said an aged clergyman:

"I notice that very many of these requests, sent in here, are for the children of pious parents; many are from pious widows for their sons. I want to say to all such, never give up your hope and confidence in a covenant-keeping God. He is a faithful God, and He keeps His promise that He will be a God to His children, and to their seed after them. And now, in order to make you understand what I mean, I will relate to you what has been said of a man who had the good news sent to him that his son, who was absent, had been converted. His informant, who expected that he would be very much excited and overjoyed, was disappointed at his calmness, and supposed some one else had informed him of the conversion of his son. So he said to him:

"'Who told you that your son was converted?'

"He replied, 'God told me. He did not tell me He had converted my son, but He told me He would convert him, and I expected it. I believed Him, and I am not surprised that He has kept His word.'

"I would say to every one of these pious-praying mothers who send their requests that we pray that their children may be converted, 'Don't give up your hope in God.'"

A gentleman said he was in the habit of attending

a little prayer-meeting held in New Haven, every Saturday night. It was a little company, like a family gathering, wherein those who attended might make known their wants with confidence.

On a late occasion a father presented the case of his son for prayer. So far as the son was concerned the case was very unpromising, for he was very reckless. When the father had presented his son for prayer he wished all in the meeting to pledge themselves to pray for his conversion. One said: "I will pray for him;" and another said "I will;" and this was repeated until all had pledged themselves to prayer. This was all within a short time past. The following Saturday that father appeared in the meeting, and said that their prayers had been answered. The night before, he said, that son had called him up at two o'clock in the morning, and begged him to pray for him. "I found him in great distress of mind. He was in agony. Of course I could do no less than spend the remaining portion of the night in praying for his conversion. Before the morning the change had taken place, and that proud heart had been humbled at the foot of the Cross." This father said he had no doubt of his son's conversion, and he believed it was in answer to prayer.

A young man arose and said he had been in the

meeting but a few times. He did not live in New York; but in coming to the city he had attended the meeting, and desired to tell the story of his conversion. He continued:

"It was not here that I was converted, but away in my Western home. I acknowledge however that I was converted in answer to prayer offered here, —for my friends sent their requests to you that this meeting would pray for my salvation. I knew nothing of their action. But when you prayed, I was smitten with the most pungent conviction of sin. I found no peace till I found it in believing. No more shall I doubt the power of prayer. I feel my great obligation to this meeting. I heard how you prayed for me. I ask that you will never be weary of praying in answer to these requests. What would have become of me if you had never prayed for me? for I was far away from my Father's house."

A gentleman spoke of the late conversion of a son of one of the most pious of mothers. She had prayed for him all her life. But she had to obey the summons, "Come up higher." She soared away to her home in the heavens with the most sublime faith in her dying hour that her son would be converted. She departed some time since. But God had not forgotten His promise. He keeps covenant with His people—a covenant well ordered in all things and sure. News came to the meeting that this son had been converted. He prays in his family—prays in the prayer-meeting, speaks in the meetings, and is active in religious duties.

"It was a singular way to answer a mother's prayers, and the prayers of this meeting,—for I believe your prayers had something to do in the great change in my brother. Your prayers had been laid up in heaven for him. God began by converting some of his children, and then, as we trust, converted him."

The same speaker continued:

"Now here is a mother asking prayer for the conversion of her son. She has come here and presented her request in person. I want to say to her, let the matter of his salvation *be settled to-day*. Give that child up to God by the exercise of a confidence in Jesus, which never goes unrewarded, and He shall say to your heart, here in this place of prayer, according to your faith, so be it unto thee."

In accordance with this mother's request earnest prayer was offered by the meeting for the conversion of her son.

A missionary's wife in South Africa, having heard of the wonderful answers God has given to prayers offered in the meeting, earnestly entreated continued supplication for her two eldest sons, now growing into manhood, that they may soon be converted, and become fully consecrated to the Saviour.

The following came from Treasure Hill, Nevada:

"My Dear Christian Friends: Though I have never seen one of your faces, yet I feel familiar with you. Yes, for ten years I have been reading of the great and marvellous work that God has used you as instruments in doing. Indeed, it has refreshed and fed my poor soul for three years here in this ungodly place, where we have no man of God to minister the bread of life to us. But my heart has been strengthened by your labors of love and faith, so that I may indeed say God has poured His Spirit upon me since the week of prayer. I now observe the hours with you, and my heart has been drawn out in heartfelt prayer for the cause of Christ in such a manner that I can spend an hour in my chamber in wrestling prayer. This spirit, my friends, is in answer to your prayers. In August last I sent a request in behalf of my husband—also for a deep work of grace in my own heart. I *know* you prayed for us. His skeptical views gave way and he joined me in prayer, and soon rejoiced in hope in Christ Jesus, in our own home. But now he longs for a deeper work of grace in his own heart. Will you now pray for him again, and ask God to give him more grace and faith in his heart?

"And, oh! be pleased to hear me in behalf of my son. I sent a request three years ago that he might be returned home from roaming around the world. His mind was fixed upon travelling. He left the college in Illinois, went on board of a ship, and was gone a year. From his letters I found he was becoming more and more fascinated with a sea-faring life. I then appealed to you. God heard your prayers. He was in a most miraculous manner saved from a watery grave, when all on board were lost, far from his home. He asked God to help him home, which He did in a few months—with no more desire to go to sea. But now he is a young man in business in San Francisco, where sin abounds in *high places*, and he is now being led by his young friends to go to the theatre and to break God's holy Sabbath.

"Oh! pray God to pour out his Holy Spirit upon him until the voice of a new-born soul may be heard praising God for His mercy. Dear friends, the hot tears of gratitude flowed to know that God answered your prayers for me and mine. Again, pray for me, that I may work for perishing souls around me here. Yours in Christian faith."

A clergyman arose and said:

"I am from the West. I want you to pray for my children. They are obedient children. They would be shocked if they should be deprived of the privilege of repeating their prayers at night and of going to the Sunday School on the Sabbath; but they are not Christians. I want you to pray for their conversion. And to encourage the hearts of fathers and mothers here, I want to relate the facts of a case of conversion which lately took place in Cincinnati.

"The son of an Eastern clergyman proved perverse and disobedient; and though an only child, he forsook his parents and wandered away into that city. His father and mother were persons of devoted piety, and never ceased to pray for their wandering boy, though they knew not where he was. The son, one evening in sauntering through the streets of the city, passed a church in which was going forward a very interesting series of meetings, which shared richly in the effusions of the Holy Spirit. He passed before the door of the church, heard the voices of singing and prayer, and all at once made up his mind that he would go in. It was a crowded prayer meeting. He advanced half way up the aisle, and stood looking on the scenes with mere idle curiosity. Of a sudden that young man became overwhelmed with deep conviction of sin, and he sank down upon the floor. The praying people gathered around him, consoled him, prayed for him, and the young man went out of that church a renewed and changed creature. He had been overtaken by surprising grace.

"He immediately sat down and wrote to his parents of the great change. He confessed and bewailed his past unkindness and disobedience, and told them that as soon as he could earn money enough to pay his expenses he would come home, and he would never leave them any more. He sent away the letter. As soon as the mail could return, it brought a letter from his mother. It expressed a mother's great joy at what the Lord had done for him. It stated to him that when he should return he would not find his father—that at the very hour when he said he was struck down with conviction of sin his father was dying, and he spent the dying hour in calling on God to have mercy on his son. His last words were a prayer for his prodigal boy.

"Thus," added the speaker, "we see how faithful God is to hear and answer prayer according to His own promise and grace. There may be despairing hearts here, doubtful about the conversion of their children whom they know they have consecrated to God. Why should they doubt? Be not faithless, but believing."

A young man said he could perceive from the prayers that had been made that there were awakened sinners in the room. He wanted to tell them that coming to Christ was easy, when we would do nothing else but come—and come now. There was no coming, in resolving to come—none in setting some future time for coming. He had seen his own mistakes, and he wished them to see theirs—and do nothing but come, and come to Him now. There was a quiet earnestness in his whole manner that went to every heart. The tears were falling all around. There was no mistaking who this young man was—the son of a veteran missionary, forty years on a mission field. This young man was the last of a large family of children who had all been gathered into the fold of the Great Shepherd. He came now to make the last straying one brought in. Some of his family are away in the missionary field. And this young man had several times, within a few months, been presented for the prayers of the meeting.

Another young man spoke as follows:

"There were five of us, left fatherless, to the care of a most devoted Christian mother. She read some accounts of answers to prayer as given in this meeting. She called me to her one day and said, 'Now I am encouraged. Here are some wonderful answers to prayer. I am going to pray for the conversion of all of you, my five dear children, just like this, and like Jacob, I will take no denial till all of you are in the kingdom.' And, sure enough, she did pray until we were all enlisted in the service of Christ. And now, here I am in this place of prayer, reading of which, she learned to trust in God."

A father asked prayer for his children. When speaking of his daughters his voice trembled. He said:

"My children have a mother who is emphatically a praying mother. We both are in a state of great anxiety for them. Our two oldest daughters are professors of religion, but are wedded to the fashionable follies of the day. I don't know whether they are Christians or not. I cannot understand what the religion is of those who are more fond of the dancing-party than they are of the praying assembly, and can go and spend almost the entire night in dancing, and show that they love those places of festivity more than they love the places where prayer is wont to be made."

Earnest prayer was offered accordingly.

A missionary mother sent all the way from India for prayer for the conversion of her son, and now she calls for thanksgiving that the Lord has heard her cry and ours. She desires the meeting now to pray that God will dispose his heart to the missionary work on the field where she labors.

A gentleman holding a book in his hand entitled "Hours of Prayer," said:

"I wish to say for the encouragement of the faith of a mother who has just asked prayers for an only son, that four years ago this very day I stood by the dying bed of one of the most devoted, praying mothers. She never was within the reach of this meeting, and yet she was profited by it beyond most others by reading the published accounts of it, by means of which she rose to a high degree of faith and trust in God. She had two unconverted sons, for whose salvation she had long prayed. When she was drawing near to her last hour, I asked her about her hope of heaven: 'Oh!' said she, 'I have come sadly short of my duty to my dear Saviour, but He can never say to me, I never knew you. He knows me and I know Him.'

"'How about your two unconverted sons?' She replied: 'That is all settled. They will be converted, and we shall be in heaven together by and by. Jesus has given me assurance of that. There is no doubt about it—all settled.' She spoke with her face radiant with joy. She went away to her heavenly home with full assurance of meeting all her children there.

"She sent a request to this meeting for prayer for the salvation of these very sons. It is recorded here in this book. Now they are both rejoicing in Christ."

On this occasion "Prayer answered" was the prominent topic of remark, as well as the principal exercise. The leader spoke as follows:

"Not long since an anxious mother in Saratoga county became very much agonized with desire for the salvation of her two sons, both of them heads of families, and both living at a distance from her, and from each other. She begged a friend to write an urgent request to this meeting for earnest prayer that her two sons might be converted. That request came in due time, and the man who wrote it kept watch of it. He knew the day and the hour it came here; he knew when it was read to the meeting; he knew that it took deep hold when it was read, and that the prayer which followed was fervent. So much he knew, but he could go no further in this direction. In another direction he made inquiries, and he found this state of facts. We mention them to the praise and glory of God's grace in answering prayer.

"The same day at night that these brothers and sons of the anxious mother were prayed for, this meeting, without the knowledge of each other, and without knowing that they had been made the subjects of prayer here, they called their families around them and set up the family altar and commenced the observance of family prayer, and thus made open confession of their faith in Jesus Christ. This illustrates the power of believing prayer. Faith must have been exercised somewhere, by the mother or this meeting, or both, and God answered the prayer of faith, by whomsoever offered."

A careless young man was found in the meeting. He had just dropped in out of curiosity. He had never been in before. After the meeting was over he fell into the company of a young man who watches for souls as one who must give account. He always carries in his pocket a small Bible, the reading of which, sometimes, does wonderful execution. On this occasion he drew the Bible from his pocket and read to him a part of the 53d chapter of Isaiah. The young man was smitten with the truth. The word was quick and powerful, sharper than a two-edged sword. It pierced his heart with amazing power, and he came at once into obedience to Christ. He wrote a letter to his father, who afterwards, with tears and sobs, read it to the meeting. This father had asked prayer for him. The mother was confined to her room, but she rejoiced over her new-born son with exceeding joy. The letter was a very touching account of one who had almost at the moment of first conviction passed from death unto life. It was wonderful grace.

"Not good enough to go to Jesus! Not good enough? The idea of fitness is nowhere to be found in the Bible."

The speaker was a young man lately from Scotland, who came into the meeting in great distress of mind, and here gained relief in finding Christ. He continued:

"This not good enough is the suggestion of the devil. It is a delusion of the arch enemy of souls. Fit to go to Jesus you can never be, and yet freely you may go with the assurance that no door shall be shut against you. Come, then, to Jesus, as you are now. There is no time for delay. Your warrant is in your very wants and your unfitness to go to Him. Your plea must be Christ's merits. May God bless you. Say, 'Make haste unto me, O God! O Lord! make no tarrying.' This is the promise on which I rested, 'And ye shall seek me and find me, when ye shall search for me with all your hearts.'"

Such as the following often reach the meeting. This request was written in a beautiful hand:

"A sorrowing mother, who has once before sent a request for prayer to the Fulton Street meeting in behalf of an only son, entreats them again to plead with the Almighty for his sake. Left fatherless, just as he grew to manhood, with plenty of means, he fell into evil company, and became dissipated. My earnest expostulations with him induced him to leave off for a time. He took the pledge of total abstinence, and I hoped he was saved. But in a few months he met an old associate who induced him again to taste of the intoxicating cup.

"He seems penitent, and again promises to abstain. But unless God helps him he will again fall into the hands of his adversaries.

"Oh! pray that he may be converted, leave off

sinning against God, and be saved from the curse of intemperance and vice."

When will such requests cease to come? They, as a class, are more numerous than any other. They come from everywhere. Shall we despair of the poor drunkard? None but God, by His converting power, can save him and keep him from falling. This sorrowing mother is right in asking for prayer for her son's repentance. He must have that repentance which is unto life, and then cast himself on Jesus, and then he will have effectual help. Prayer was fervent for him.

The meeting was near closing when one after another had requested that their friends and neighbors might be remembered in prayer. The chairman was just rising, when a gentleman said:

"Will you hear me a moment, Mr. Chairman? I saw a poor German boy come in here, a youth 20 years of age, bringing in his mother with him, as I suppose. That boy is in great distress of mind. He has been here day after day for many days past, and I ask you to pray for his conversion now,—immediately. He longs to be a Christian. He is very earnest in his seeking after Christ. We prayed with him yesterday. He asked us if he could take his sins back. I do not know what he meant by that. Did he mean to recall them? I have since been thinking of it. Did he mean if he might confess them? Did he mean if he might renounce them? We may not be able to understand him or teach him, but we can pray that the Holy Spirt may teach him; for He can understand him and He can teach without the least error."

The meeting then united in fervent prayer, in which this youth was remembered, with special interest, that he might understand and accept salvation as offered in the Gospel. At the close of the services we conversed and prayed with him again. The conversation was partly in English and partly in German. We inquired what he meant when he asked the day before "if he could take his sins back." He answered:

"Some few days ago I thought I had suffered enough, and I told God that I did not want anything more to do with Him. Now I want to take that back. I want Him to forgive me. I shall have very much to do with Him if He will let me take that back. I am so sorry I said it."

He was told certainly he could take that back; if he felt that he had done wrong, and wanted to be forgiven, all he had to do was to go to God and tell Him just how he felt about it, and ask to be forgiven through Christ, and he must be sorry for this and all his sins, and God would forgive him. He seemed to be greatly rejoiced when told that even so great a sin could be forgiven, if he was truly sorry for it, and would trust in Christ as the Saviour of sinners. Then followed a conversation in the German language which he could more readily understand. It was held both with him and his mother.

A hardware merchant next addressed the Chairman, who was also a hardware merchant. Said he:

"I think we do not often enough remember to give thanks in this meeting for what God is doing and has done for us. We please Him as much in our thankfulness as in our earnestness in prayer. I should like to have these petitioners tell us how the Lord has blessed them, and call upon us to render praise and thanksgiving to Him for the benefits bestowed. A short time ago, I asked you to pray for my sick son. He is well now, sir. He is well; he is in heaven. He died a most happy Christian, rejoicing in the Saviour. He sunk down and down, bearing his testimony all along down into the valley, of the blessedness of the love of Christ. His death was a triumph over death. We watched him as far as we could see him. We could see him passing on and on, through the valley and into the water flood. But the cold river is past now, sir. He is on the shining shore. I want to call on this meeting to render thanks to God for His merciful kindness in bearing my son safely through, and taking him home to heaven."

All the time the father's eyes were suffused with tears, and his voice trembled with deep emotion, showing that his heart was singing for joy in view of that wonderful grace that prepares a sinner for glory, and brings him off more than a conqueror. Prayer and thanksgiving followed, and then how appropriate and solemn was the singing of the hymn—

>"Our days are passing swiftly by,
> And I, a fleeting stranger,
>Would not detain them as they fly,
> Those hours of toil and danger:
>For O! we stand on Jordan's strand,
> Our friends are passing over
>And just before, the shining shore
> We may almost discover."

Here sits a plain looking lady. Some time ago, say two or three months, she wrote a letter to this meeting desiring prayers for a son whom she had not seen for twenty-four years, and had not heard from for twenty years. She had no knowledge whether he was alive or dead, or if living, in what part of the world he might be. She desired the meeting to pray that she might hear from her long lost son if alive, or be informed of his death if he had been called to another world. If living, she desired earnest prayers that he might become a Christian. Now notice how God answers prayer.

There that mother sits with three letters in her hand from that son. The first was sent to the Old World where the son supposed his mother was, and by friends forwarded to this New World, where she has long resided. Two other letters followed, when he found out where she was. And here sits the meek and quiet mother, holding in her hand these three letters, looking the very personification of happiness. She also holds in her hand a photograph of the house in which he dwells, and himself standing in the door and looking out. But, what is better than all, one of these letters informs the mother that this son has become a Christian.

The leader of the meeting, an old merchant, had looked over these proofs of answer to prayer and made statement of these facts, so encouraging to those who love to pray.

On one occasion there was a poor sinner in great distress in the meeting. While a brother was speaking, and urging home the duty of repentance, he burst forth into the cry, "Oh, what shall I do to be saved?" We looked in the direction of the sound, and there the man was—on his knees—begging for mercy. Another near him rose and asked the meeting to sing for him—the tears, meanwhile, streaming down his cheeks—

"Rock of Ages, cleft for me,
Let me hide myself in Thee."

After meeting, these men were conversed with privately, and directed to come at once to Christ with all their load of guilt upon them—for they were undoubtedly very wicked men.

The man who cried out in the meeting had been made the subject of prayer before, at his own request, which was written by himself, and was as follows:

"The prayers of this meeting are respectfully requested for G. B——, who has lived all his life in wickedness, and only a few days ago contemplated suicide, and the great crime of murder, in hope of ending his misery."

The writer asked this man if he really did intend to commit murder, and then suicide.

"I really did," said he.

"Whom did you intend to murder?"

"A woman who has greatly wronged me; and to be revenged I intended to kill her!"

"And what then?"

"Suicide, and eternal damnation."

"Have you any such feelings now?"

"Not the least."

"What saved you from the crimes you intended to commit?"

"The recollection of my poor mother's prayers."

And now his chin quivered, and his eyes filled with tears.

"Have you ever committed a crime, and been imprisoned?" we continued.

"Never," said he, with great emphasis and firmness—and we believed him.

This man has been present at nearly all the meetings, and now hopes that his sins have been washed away in the blood of Him who has said that He can save to the uttermost all such as come unto God through Him.

CHAPTER XVIII.

VARIOUS OPERATIONS OF THE HOLY SPIRIT.

The answers to prayer are not always in the way and manner that the believer expects, but these records prove that believing prayer is heard.

A gentleman, a member of a church in Brooklyn, said:

"I have often asked you to pray for the conversion of my children. Now I have the satisfaction of telling you that out of the five, I have four praying children, and I believe the fifth will soon be converted.

"I have often asked you to pray for the outpouring of the Holy Spirit upon the church, and I have known as many as fifty-one praying wives praying for the conversion of their impenitent husbands, and I have seen many of those husbands converted. Oh! God does hear and answer prayer. How I have reason for thanksgiving for what He has done for me and mine."

One writes from Michigan, saying he sent here for prayer for the outpouring of the Holy Spirit upon himself and his people. He says he does not know that it has ever been received, but he presumes it has, for the Lord is pouring out His Spirit in great power, and more than seventy souls have been converted. He says to the meeting, "Do pray again and again for us that God will continue and extend this mighty work of grace, and pour His blessed Spirit all abroad."

A lady writes to the meeting a most joyful letter, giving thanks to God that He has heard prayer in her behalf—a poor, despairing sinner—and now she is happy in the Lord.

"Jesus, I my cross have taken,
All to leave and follow Thee,"

is the language of her glad heart.

Thanksgiving as well as prayer is called for every week, by some who send requests, as in the following:

"God has heard and answered prayer in many of the petitions which I have sent, asking the supplications of the meeting from time to time. Oh, magnify His grace with me. Still pray for the conversion of my two sons and their father."

Another, evidently written by a pastor, says:

"Beloved Brethren and Sisters in the Lord—Some weeks ago a request was sent to you asking you to pray for a work of grace in Schuylerville, Saratoga county. About one week ago some special services were begun here with Christians of different denominations, which have been honored of God in a revival and religious awakening. The love and zeal of God's people have been greatly and strongly warmed, and careless and prayerless sinners have been converted by repentance and faith in Christ. Children as well as adults have been brought to believe in Jesus, and others are seriously reflecting on their spiritual state. A daily prayer-meeting has been held at 8 A. M., since the close of the preaching services, with very blessed effect. Christians are refreshed by it, and stimulated to work for the Saviour, and for souls, throughout the day. Oh, will you not unite with us in thanksgiving to God, and in prayer that we may not be weary in well-doing?"

A speaker said:

"A few years ago a few ladies met in New Haven to pray for the outpouring of the Holy Spirit. The result was a revival of religion that spread over the town, that swept through the college, and prevailed all around. This was some years ago. Twenty-five of my class-mates were converted, all of whom entered the ministry. Some have occupied high and exalted stations of usefulness. All have been the blessed instruments of winning many souls to Jesus. Some have gone to their reward. Others still live to gather the sheaves into the garner of the Lord. I speak only of the converted in my own class. Oh! who will tell me where ends the influence of that little, unostentatious ladies' prayer-meeting? When in answer to their prayers the college, the town, the region of country round about was roused out of sleep by the coming of the Holy Spirit. Who can tell?"

The same speaker said:

"It is told of Dr. Lyman Beecher that he once prayed in his study for a revival of religion among his people, and he found such liberty in prayer that he prayed all night. It was prayer for the outpouring of the Holy Spirit. The heavenly rain descended in copious effusions, like the rain that waters all the plain. In going from house to house he found another who had prayed all night long for the same blessing. Multitudes were converted, and among them some of the shining lights of the day."

A minister from Rochester, N. Y., said:

"We know God hears and answers prayer. But whose prayers are heard and answered in any particular case, we never can tell. Some three months ago one of the elders in one of our Presbyterian churches made some statements in the prayer-meeting in regard to how God hears and answers prayer, and stated some facts which he had gathered from the reports of the religious press. He proposed that we should ask your prayers for the outpouring of the Holy Spirit upon our churches of Rochester. I know you prayed for us. Wonderfully has God answered somebody's prayers. We have had a glorious work of grace, and we have added to our churches two hundred and twenty-five on profession of their faith in Jesus, and the end is not yet. Your prayers and ours, and those of others, have together prevailed with God, and so we are encouraged to pray and believe."

The meeting was led one day by an educated Irish layman. He spoke of the wide-spread influence of this meeting, as he stood holding in his hand a request from London, which he was about to read. He expressed the hope that the object presented for prayer would be earnestly remembered. The request ran as follows:

"LONDON, ENGLAND, }
April, 17, 1871. }

"DEAR BRETHREN IN THE LORD:

"Your prayers are asked for God's special·blessing upon the preaching of the Gospel, now about to commence in our tent upon the London fields and in the lecture-room in connection therewith. Also thank the Lord, with us, for the great blessing given to our efforts during the last season's services. Please to keep this matter before you always, when you approach the mercy seat. 'If two of you shall agree on earth, touching anything that they shall ask, it shall be done for them of my Father which is in heaven.

"Yours truly,   J. E."

Upon another day a gentleman from Philadelphia said he brought the salutations of the daily meeting of their city to this, and specially invited this to join them in earnest prayer for the outpouring of the Holy

Spirit upon the churches. He said that the churches of Philadelphia had agreed to set apart a day of special prayer, from 10 A. M., to 10 P. M., for the outpouring of the Holy Spirit. He was urgent that we should pray that this day of prayer might be followed with the most abundant blessings. It was a touching appeal that we would help them by our prayers to prepare the way of the Lord.

Another gentleman arose and said he was from Boston, and he brought the salutations of the Boston daily prayer-meeting. He said the one great, grave, and deep impression upon all minds is this—that we are on the eve of a great revival—a greater revival than the world has ever witnessed before. All the providences of God through which the world is passing are leaning to it. God is preparing His own way by the sore judgments which He is sending upon the nations. He has taken his glittering sword. He has made ready his bow. He will thresh the nations in His anger if they do not repent. These are the signs of His coming by His Spirit to gather in His garner His chosen. The speaker continued:

"We are looking for great displays of His grace. We beg an interest in your prayers. Let us join our prayers with those of thousands who are praying for the displays of the power of the Spirit. With the stripes administered by one hand, he comes with the pot of honey in the other. God chastens but to save."

The hour of the meeting was mostly spent in very earnest, ardent prayer. More than one would arise at the same time to engage in prayer. A gentleman arose several times, and would be partly up when he would hear the voice of some one, and would resume his seat. He looked like a clergyman. He was polished and scholarly in his appearance, and was evidently a stranger, and did not know how prompt he must be in order to get the floor. He sat with tears in his eyes during the last half hour. We supposed he had some intelligence he wished to communicate.

"What did you wish to say?" we ventured to ask, as he turned to go, on the close of the benediction.

"I wished to pray," said the gentleman.

"Are you a clergyman?"

"Yes, and I wanted to lead in prayer for the outpouring of the Holy Spirit upon my people. I intended to state my desire, and then I wanted to pray."

"Well, you have prayed. Your desire is prayer. Do you believe God will grant the desire of your heart?"

"I am sure He will. I know He will. I have never been in this meeting before. But I shall go home with heavenly benedictions in my heart, and I shall preach and pray in the spirit of this hour, and I am sure God will hear and answer."

Near the close of another meeting a young man had arisen and said: "In January last I was here for the first time. I asked your prayers for my Sunday-school. Since that time forty scholars in that Sunday-school have been converted."

Another was deeply affected when he began to speak. He said:

"I have been sick, and I got my friends to write a request for prayer and sent it here for your supplications in my behalf. I was unconverted. Nobody thought I could live. But God had mercy on my soul. Oh, what mercy! I was on the brink of the Jordan of death. I expected to pass over every moment. But I assure you I found the waters divided. I should have passed over on dry land. But God called me back. I am here in answer to prayer; spared for a little time to work for Jesus. Oh, how I loved Him! How I wish others to love Him!"

He sat down weeping like a child.

A young man sent the following to the leader's table:

"A professor of religion has allowed himself, since his recent arrival in the city, to be controlled by the tempter, by joining company with sinful companions, and has followed them in the forbidden paths of vice. He has been arrested in his sinful career by the Spirit of a merciful God, and with an aching heart and troubled mind he solicits the prayers of this meeting on his behalf, that he may find forgiveness, peace, and reconciliation with his all-wise and merciful Saviour."

This request was followed with prayer that was answered on the spot, according to Scripture promise: "While they are yet speaking I will hear." For at the close of the meeting the young man who wrote this came up to the missionary of the meeting and said, "I now feel happy in believing in Christ." The next day he gave some account of the experience he had passed through, and exhorted sinners to come directly to Christ. A young man had been up before him and expressed an earnest desire to become a Christian. "Now," said he, "let that young man just go to Jesus and he will find a welcome just as I have done, and the assurance fulfilled, 'Though your sins be as scarlet they shall be whiter than snow, and though they be red like crimson they shall be as wool.'" This he felt had been fulfilled in his case.

Another fact may be mentioned of great interest: A town in Pennsylvania had sent an earnest request for prayer, which entered deeply into the supplications of the meeting. It was from a pastor and people that the Holy Spirit may be poured out upon them in copious effusions. A telegram came from this place, as follows:

"*To the Fulton Street Prayer Meeting, New York*:

"Scores of converts—Christians working and travailing for souls. Pray again for the hundreds unconverted.

This excited great interest in the hearts of those present, and earnest prayer was offered.

At one meeting nine young men who have lately set out on a religious life, each in a few words told the story of his religious experience. Five, one right after the other, gave in their testimony for Jesus, and told of their love and faith in Him. Another was standing on the floor when the leader said, "Let some-one now pray, and after prayer these testimonies may proceed." When prayer had been offered, four more, in twice as many minutes, told what the Lord had done for their souls. The meeting was very much moved, and melted under the power of these testimonies.

Said a speaker:

"Oh that we might have hearts to call down upon the churches the richest of heaven's blessings. It sometimes seems that we were never so needy as now. Is it a question whether we shall have revivals in our churches this fall and winter. We have something to do to have this question rightly settled. If we will pray, and believe, we shall surely see the wonderful works of God in the salvation of souls. We cannot *pray* in vain for the outpouring of the Holy Spirit. No amount of talking about the need of such an unspeakable blessing will bring it. It goes not out but by prayer and fasting. We must humble ourselves before God. We must pray out of the dust. We must come back to God from all our backslidings of heart and life. We must have the spirit of true and unfeigned repentance. We must pray in faith."

The leader of the meeting was a Presbyterian clergyman. He said he came to the work of the ministry in this city seven years ago. One of the first things he did was to come to this prayer-meeting and ask prayer for a revival of religion. And that winter they gathered over one hundred into their church, who were converted, as he believed, in answer to prayer. "Now," he added, "I come again to ask you to pray for us: for we, as a church, long to see the work of God revive, and sinners converted to Christ."

A Presbytery in Central Ohio sent to the meeting an earnest request for prayer that the influences of the Holy Spirit might be shed down upon them and all their churches. They stated in their communication that, on the same day that prayer should be offered here, they would spend the entire day in earnest supplication at the mercy-seat for the rain of heavenly grace to be poured upon them.

The leader said he had come from a meeting of ten or twelve Presbyterian ministers and two or three Reformed. They had spent an hour together in prayer, and many tears were shed. This was not the first of the kind; others had preceded it of the same nature, and for the same objects. At their last meeting some reported an awakened interest, and in two churches several had requested prayer for themselves; and they were greatly encouraged.

Said a French clergyman:

"It is two years since I had the pleasure of being in this meeting. My present field of labor is among the French Roman Catholics of New England. There are one hundred and fifty thousand of them in these States. Until lately nothing has been done to meet their spiritual wants. I find them everywhere easy of access. Thirty years ago I was converted by means of reading the Romish version of the New Testament. There is now a French version, approved by the present Pope. I believe there is enough of the Gospel in it to lead a sinner to Christ, and I give that where I can give no other. Last Sabbath, in Salem, I was told there were no Roman Catholics in the place. I did not expect an audience of more than fifty persons, though I knew there were some there. But, to my surprise, 200 French Roman Catholics were present. I have a large and scattered field. My plan is to endeavor to win some to Christ; and when converted—two or three in a place—I immediately organize them into a little band for work, and holding meetings among their people and carrying on the work of evangelization till churches can be organized. We have now several churches, and in them 10,000 converts to the true faith."

Another bore witness to the willingness of Roman Catholics to listen to the truth. These are not Irish

Catholics, nor are they like them. When approached in kindness they can appreciate it, and are won by it.

Some weeks before a minister wrote to the meeting, asking prayer for the influences of the Holy Spirit upon the hearts of those among whom he was about to establish preaching services. It was a place in Macon county, Ill., destitute of religious privileges. The case was presented to the meeting, and taken up with earnest supplication for the outpouring of the Holy Spirit upon the efforts which were to be made for the salvation of souls. In a few weeks came the following, under date of November 3, 1871:

"Dear Christians—Praise ye the Lord. The Lord has answered prayer, and fifteen have been converted, and I have organized them into a church."

This was the substance. Again he writes, after a few more days:

"Praise ye the Lord. He has done great things for us. Our little band is trebled. We have had wonderful manifestations of saving power. The most notoriously profane man in this region has had a new song put into his mouth; even praise to our God. Numbers have sought the prayers of Christians. The meeting has continued nearly six weeks without any diminution of interest. Our large school-house cannot hold the people. Shall this work cease? I am willing to work on. We beg you to continue your prayers for us. I send you the names of forty individuals—young, middle-aged, and aged males and females—for whom I ask you to pray for their immediate conversion. I retain a copy of this list of names, and will report to you the results. May God bless you for your past interest, and dispose you to pray without ceasing. Sabbath week I propose to hold a communion season with this new organization. Pray for us."

Afterward came the following communication:

"By God's blessing I am able to report an organization of over fifty members of the church, and a fair prospect of building a house of worship the next summer. Some, whose names I placed on a list to you, have already professed a change of heart. For a short time these meetings will be suspended. The people need rest. I propose to rest by engaging in another meeting. God seems to be preparing the way by His providential dealings. Pray for us. Pray for me that we may have a great blessing. "Pastor."

In one of the meetings an earnest Christian thus gave utterance to his feelings and experience. Said he:

"We need such a measure of faith and prayer that nothing can hinder a revival of religion, one continuous shower of the rain of heavenly grace, when conversions shall be multiplied as the drops of the morning. We must have such holy living and such overcoming, prevailing faith that shall enlist divine and infinite mercy and love in the salvation of the world, and then we shall see the light of the milennial glory.

"I knew a church years ago which was formed of eleven members in the midst of a godless manufacturing people; and these eleven members entered into a solemn covenant with each other that they would live for a perpetual revival of religion, and a constant ingathering of souls. What was the result? Four large churches gathered, and their own increased to 500 or 600 members.

"Thirteen years afterward I met one of the original eleven, away out on the banks of the Mississippi, at St. Louis. He went into their church prayer-meeting. It was Rev. Dr. Bullard's. He told the simple story of his life with Jesus. All hearts melted like wax before the fire. To have a revival of religion you must have one man on fire; and that fire will kindle another, and so it will spread from heart to heart. I heard of this same man in other places, and always I find the same glorious results to follow. Men would get awake to their spiritual interests because they could not help it when in contact with such a man. Shall we have such men in the churches? Shall we have such churches? Some anxious souls were in this meeting. They gathered around a little knot of ministers and others, to whom they told their anxiety. At length one said, 'Let us pray,' and all knelt on the floor, and three prayers were offered. Then the voice of one young man was heard, consecrating himself to Jesus in an everlasting covenant never to be forgotten. All who heard that prayer of a few words believed that the destiny of a soul turned on those few words uttered with all the heart."

The Week of Prayer in 1872 was very fruitful in the spiritual blessings, having been followed by continual prayer in the churches for a mighty outpouring of the Holy Spirit. Many churches began daily meetings before the week, as if they felt sure that a blessing would come, and they desired to be prepared for it. And the blessing did come in a most signal manner. Before this, many seemed discouraged on account of the abounding demoralization of the times. But no sooner had churches began to pray than God began to bless in answering prayer. Christians were quickened, and sinners were awakened and converted. The old revival spirit returned, and the cords of Zion were lengthened, and her stakes were strengthened, proving that nothing is too hard for God.

Said a speaker:

"At Ellenville, in the M. E. Church, a most animating sight was presented last Sabbath. It was communion Sabbath. The scene was impressive and affecting when, after a sermon by the pastor, setting forth the evidences of a change of heart, ninety-two came forward for admittance into the church. They embraced all classes and conditions, varying in their ages from twelve to seventy years. These are among the number who have been hopefully converted during a series of meetings began weeks ago, and which are still continued. Others are expected to take the same step at a future time, and some are going or have gone into other churches. Many more are anxiously inquiring after the way of eternal life. A marked feature of this religious awakening is the work of grace in the Sabbath-school, where it had its beginning, and where it has been a wonderful power to lead souls to believe in Jesus. In the Reformed church, also, this work of grace has been going on for some time past, and many have professed their faith in Christ, and many more are saying, 'Men and brethren, what shall we do?' We ask you to pray for the continuance and enlargement of this work."

A precious revival is in progress in Vincentown, where over thirty have been hopefully converted. A wonderful change has taken place there, and in the surrounding country. A few months ago many miserable children had little to eat and little to wear, on account of the drunkenness of their fathers, who were never seen in the house of God. But now they have sober, industrious fathers, with plenty to eat and to wear; and on the Sabbath day, fathers and mothers, and children, are found sitting happily together in the house of God. A little over a year ago there were three rum-shops in the town, where liquor was sold or given away; and on Saturday nights the town was in an uproar till a late hour, by reason of the noise of drunken carousals. Now the rum-shops are closed, and the town is peaceful at all hours of the day and night. It is an amazing change.

NO SUCH REVIVAL IN FORTY YEARS.

A speaker said:

"I reside forty miles from this city in a suburban village, on which there has been a gracious outpouring of the Holy Spirit, resulting in a most glorious work of divine grace. It commenced with the Week of Prayer. Such a revival has not been known in the township in forty years. The churches of all denominations have shared in the blessing."

After prayer, a gentleman from Philadelphia said that one of the requests read had deeply moved his heart. It was the request for a class of little boys. He was reminded of a little boy in the Sunday-school of which he was the superintendent, only twelve years old. Said he:

"And, on looking round the room—strange as it may seem—I see the young man present who was the teacher of that little boy in the Sunday-school. To show you how important it is that we do with all our might what we can, for the dear little boys, let me tell you about Mattie ——. He had no pious father or mother to encourage him or to teach him how to become a Christian. But from the beginning of his coming to the school he seemed to be anxious—so much so, that he would be always there, and always at the prayer-meetings appointed in connection with the school. Often you might see the big tears rolling down his cheek, and say to him, Mattie, what is the matter? He would answer, 'Oh! I am so anxious to become a Christian!'

"One night he had been over to the church, at the prayer-meeting. On coming home, his mother said: 'Why, Mattie, where have you been all this time?'

"'I have been at the church, mother,' he replied.

"'Well,' said she, with an impatient manner, 'I think, hereafter, you might as well live over at the church, Mattie.'

"The poor boy looked up, with his eyes suffused in tears, and a deeply wounded spirit, and said: 'Oh! mother, I am so anxious that you should become a Christian, and father too, and myself.'

"So he continued to seek and to strive, and we did all we could to bring him to embrace the Saviour, as He is offered in the gospel. Some time since he seemed to have found comfort and peace.

"A few days ago, poor Mattie was on his way home from his day-school, and was run over by the railroad cars and was killed. He only lived seven minutes from the time he was struck. When the train stopped, one wheel was resting on his body. They backed the train off from him, inquired of him who he was and where he lived, and received from him his last messages to his parents, and then he was gone! We learned that he did all this with the most perfect composure. We may hope that now he is gone to be forever with that Saviour whom he had anxiously sought."

The young gentleman arose, who said he was the teacher of Mattie. He had been from Philadelphia to Boston; and, being on his way back, he thought he would come into the Fulton Street Prayer Meeting—little thinking that he was here to learn, for the first time, the death of Mattie ———. The last thing he did, before leaving Philadelphia, was to attend a prayer-meeting. Mattie was there, and sat beside him; and, as the meeting went on, he leaned his head upon his shoulder, weeping all the time, and whispered to him, and said, 'Mr. A———, won't you pray for me, and ask the meeting to pray for me?'

"I immediately arose," continued the speaker, "and stated to the meeting Mattie's request, and prayed for him. After the meeting, I had a few words with him; told him I was going away; said to him that he must go to Christ, with full confidence and trust in Him, and said, as my parting words, 'When I come back, Mattie, I hope I shall find you rejoicing in a Saviour's love.' And here I learn that I shall see his face no more.

"Mattie often told me how anxious he was for his unconverted father and mother. He was the only child of the family. As I walked towards the house with him I thought I ought to go in with Mattie, and try to persuade them to come to Christ. I thought, however, I must delay it to another time? How anxious he was for me to go in, as I drew near the door. How sorry I am now that I did not! Mattie was doing his last work, and I ought to have helped him in his last labor of love. Oh! how earnest we should be for the little boys to gather them into the fold of the Good Shepherd! Oh! gather them in— gather them in!"

Several young men expressed the hope that they had been converted. In tender and touching words they gave the main facts of their Christian experience. Sometimes the meeting has been melted under the power of these facts. Very few people shed tears over falsehoods. There is a something that whispers to the heart, "This is truth:" and most glorious truth it is when a poor sinner can say, "I know in whom I have believed."

Some of these cases of late hopeful conversion have been of amazing interest. Such was the case of a young Roman Catholic. By some mysterious influence he felt moved to come into this meeting, he never could tell how. He came several times and stood on the opposite side of the street, and saw others coming in, and went away irresolute, and could not get courage to enter the meeting, till he found it required more courage to stay away. With increasing religious anxiety, he came from day to day. His friends found out the state of his mind, and took alarm at the bare possibility of his leaving the Roman Catholic Church, and joining a Catholic Church which was not Roman. They interposed their entreaties, warnings, and threatenings. When they found these had no power, then they tried the power of money. One of his friends offered him $15,000 if he would renounce his present convictions, and come back with his whole heart to the bosom of Holy Mother Church. This would not do. The more they offered, the more stoutly he resisted their offers. He felt that he could not sell his soul for gold. This young man is now rejoicing in the hope that, through Jesus Christ, the great High Priest, he has received the pardon of his sins, and has become reconciled to God.

The following is deeply affecting. A young man said:

"When I hear how the Lord blesses your prayers in the salvation of many, I beg leave to ask you again to pray for my poor brother. I have asked you once before to pray for him. He is my only brother, and I cannot see him perish without an effort on my part to save him. Although he is far from me, in Wisconsin, I feel that the Lord can reach him there. Oh, my dear friends, pray for him with all prayer and supplication; and also for me, that I may be more faithful in my Master's cause—in leading precious souls to Jesus. I also ask you to pray for one of my Sabbath-school class, whose mother is a Roman Catholic, and whose father, now dead, was a Protestant. She came to my class some time ago and expressed a desire to love Jesus. Her mother found out that she came, and whipped the poor child so that she could not rise from her bed. I dare not see her, but I learn from another of the class that she is still anxious to become a Christian. Her mother is preparing her for the nunnery. I feel very anxious about her case, and I beg an interest in all your prayers for these two cases, that they may both be brought to Jesus. Do not forget them."

No, no! they must not be forgotten. They have been and they must continue to be very earnestly remembered in prayer, that the God of all grace and consolation would appear in mercy for them. The whipping of a child, whose only crime is seeking the Lord in connection with a Protestant Sunday-school, so that she cannot rise from her bed, is nothing new or strange in Roman Catholic families. It is the old spirit of persecution, to prevent their becoming Protestants, or even Christians.

Some time ago, a young man, reared a Roman Catholic, gave an account of his own conversion, and begged the meeting to pray for him and his wife. Afterwards he said in the meeting:

"After my conversion, your prayers were requested for my wife. Yesterday intelligence was received from her that the Holy Spirit had wrought the great change in her heart, that she had given herself to the Lord Jesus, and was ready to walk with me in a new religious life."

Among many requests came the following:

"Your prayers are again requested for the young Romanist who refused to barter his liberty. His relatives, finding him proof against bribery, have deprived him of all intercourse with his Protestant friends. Thousands of miles from you this helpless soul is struggling, friendless and alone. Will you pray that he who is thus shut out from all tender advice and sympathy, may have his heart illumined, comforted, and strengthened, and that a speedy emancipation may be granted out of this bondage to sin, into the glorious liberty of sonship with Christ? Please bear him on your hearts every day, until you hear that he is safe within the fold."

This is the same young man for whom prayer was requested as being exceedingly anxious about his soul, and as having lost all confidence in the Roman Church; to whom a brother had offered $15,000 if he would renounce his convictions and return to his confidence in the Roman Church, as being the true, apostolic, Catholic Church. He has been in this meeting, and prayer was also then asked for him. It seems that he has now been spirited away beyond the reach of Protestant influences, and doomed to what we know not, by his Roman friends, whose tender mercies are cruel.

Another said:

"I am a Frenchman, I was brought up in the Roman Catholic Church; I went to the prayer-meeting, and there was no place to sit or stand, I could understand but little English. One man beckoned to me to come up on the stairs of the pulpit. I pressed along and went up. That little act of kindness took hold of my heart; I kept going. I found that all this was about coming to Christ; about giving ourselves to the Lord Jesus. The arrow sunk down into my heart, I think I want religion too; I began to pray to Jesus—I said, 'Lord Jesus, have mercy on me'—and He did have mercy on me. I wrote to France and told them what a Saviour I had found. My father wrote back and said that I was one *sacre heretic*. Since that the Lord has converted my father and mother, and now we are all heretics together."

So he went on in his narrative, in broken English, saying that in a few months God had done great things for him, and for his family at home, through the instrumentality of his letters.

The sacrament of the Lord's Supper was administered in the old Dutch Church, in Fulton Street, where the preacher and administrator was the Rev. Dr. De Witt, the senior pastor of the Collegiate church: and here a converted Roman Catholic physician sat down for the first time to the table of the Lord, and partook of the emblems of the broken body and the shed blood of our Lord and Saviour Jesus Christ. The next day the following letter was read:

"*To the Fulton Street Prayer Meeting:*

"I am a Catholic, but I have seen with deep interest the good accomplished through your powerful influence. I feel that I need the coöperation and intercession of Christian friends to assist me in the work of conversion, and therefore I solicit it for Jesus' sake, as a Christian and a sinner, even though not of your persuasion.
"ONE WHO SEEKS CONVERSION."

Another letter, also from a Roman Catholic, was read. These letters received earnest responses in prayer.

A gentleman said:

"A young lady, of this city, went about a certain neighborhood, distributing Bibles to a very poor class of French Roman Catholics. To as many as would recive it, she gave a Bible in French. Some received it, and among the rest one poor woman.

"Some days after, her brother was out on the same errand as that of the young lady—the distribution of the Bible in French—and it so happened that he went into the house of this same French woman. After being seated, she was inquired of, by the young man, whether she had a Bible. She looked at her visitor very attentively, and finally said—'Why do you ask me if I have a Bible?'

"'I only wanted to know,' said he, 'if you would like to have one.'

"'Then you are not a Catholic, are you?' she inquired.

"'No! I am not a Catholic; I am a Protestant; and I came to inquire if it would be agreeable to you to receive a Bible.'

"'Oh, sir,' said she, 'I was afraid you were a Roman Catholic, and was afraid to answer.'

"And, pulling a little Bible out of her *pocket*, she said: 'That little Bible was given me by a young lady. You will not take it from me, will you?—for it has told me I am a sinner, and led me to feel that I must have a Saviour.'

"And then, seeming to lose confidence, she burst forth with the imploring entreaty—'You will not take it from me, sir! you will not tell any of the Catholics that I have it. Don't tell them: I cannot give up my Bible, for it tells me how to come to Christ. Don't tell the priest that I have the Bible.' And with that she hid it again in her pocket."

Another gentleman said:

"I was here yesterday requesting your prayers for a Roman Catholic girl living in my family. She had for some time attended family worship, read her Bible, and of late had attended prayer-meetings. She had been very much affected by the prayers made in the family, and said that sometimes she had been so overcome that it seemed to her that she would have to leave and go out, being unable to control herself. Now I am here to ask you to unite with me in giving thanks to God for hearing prayer in that girl's conversion. She now hopes she is a Christian, and her whole countenance and manner betoken the great change which has taken place in her heart."

At another time a gentleman addressed the meeting, who is the pastor of a church on Staten Island. He is a convert from the Roman Catholic Church. He urged the duty of personal effort in bringing sinners to Christ. There is nothing like it—this preaching the gospel by fervent, earnest, personal entreaty. He said that some time ago he came to the meeting, and made request for prayer for his brothers, who were Roman Catholics, in a large business in the western part of this State. Since his own conversion, he had maintained a constant correspondence with these brothers. It had been very full of tender interest on his part, and of bitterness and coldness on theirs. Twice, within a short time past, has he requested prayer for their conversion. After the first request for prayer had been presented, he received a letter from one of these brothers, which seemed to be written in an entirely different spirit from any which he had before received. He said he had that very morning received another from this same brother, which he had a desire to read to the meeting. It gave an account of that brother's conversion. He now states that he sees the fallacy of his hopes, and that his only resting-place is the foundation of the apostles and prophets, Jesus Christ himself being the chief corner-stone. He said he had no idea, when he first began to inquire, that the foundation on which he had so long rested—namely, the Divine infallibility of the church, the Roman Catholic Church—would so soon be removed, and vanish away like the changing, shifting quicksand, so that he would be made to feel, as soon as he became an anxious inquirer after truth, that he had nothing to stand upon whatever. But so it had been. Now he trusts only to the atoning blood and righteousness of the Lord Jesus Christ.

The letter went on to entreat prayer for the remaining brothers, and an uncle, with whom this new convert from Rome had begun the work of personal duty in endeavoring to show them that there is no other foundation than that is laid, which is Jesus Christ. Said the clergyman:

"Thus you see that this personal work, which I am attempting to carry forward, begets the same kind of effort in another. I endeavor to influence my brother; he becomes converted, and he immediately endeavors to influence another's mind—and so it goes. The good we do to others, leads them to do the same work to others; and so, on and on, the work perpetuates itself, and travels down the stream of time into eternity.

"'The good, men do, lives after them.'

"The great thing wanted in the Church is personal, daily effort in persuading sinners to come to Christ."

A Catholic from the Confessional appeared in the meeting. She was a woman of, perhaps, thirty-five years of age—a widow—the mother of children in tender years. She appeared to be in deep distress. She wept bitterly, as she told to one who conversed with her, and reported the story of her sorrow, disappointment, bereavement, and, now, of religious anxiety. Her husband had been an Englishman, a Protestant, a warm-hearted, pious, devoted Christian. He had married this Catholic woman, under the promise that she should not go to the Confessional, and should leave him to enjoy his own religion without molestation. It was also stipulated that their children should follow the religious training of their father. Said the poor, weeping woman:

"I had to almost swear to him that in all this I would do as he wished. How poorly I repaid his kindness to me! We were married—I to remain a bigoted, superstitious Roman Catholic, and he a man enlightened and ennobled by his religion. He came to this country to better our condition. He sent for me to come and join him. I came to New York with the money he had sent me, only to find that I was a widow, and my children were fatherless. He had been taken away from me; and oh! sir, so sudden! And the most cutting thing of all is that he has died, and I can never undo, to him, what I have done. I can undo something of it, so far as I am concerned. But I cannot undo all." And here she burst out in bitter wailing—"I never can undo the wrong I did him. *I had our children all secretly baptized by the priest;* and he died and never knew it. This wrong I can never undo.

"We were married when I was seventeen years old. He was always very much attached to me. He had full confidence in me, but he would never yield that I should go to confession. He opposed strongly, and in this I obeyed him—though the priest was alway urging me to come. I never, before marriage, went much to confession. The last time I went was before I was twelve years old. At twelve I was confirmed. And then the next time was when I came here, and found my husband dead. I wanted some consolation. I was free, and could do as I pleased. So I entered the Confessional; and oh! how shocked and disgusted I was. Why, I would not stay. I ran out in the midst of my confessions. I told them I should go. They undertook to drag me back. But I told them, No! I would never go back—I would never enter the Confessional again. Such shocking indecency! I had heard of such things. Now I knew for myself.

"I told them that I never would enter the church again. And I never will. I am done with them forever." The poor woman spoke with great indignation. "I have read books describing the doings of wicked priests, and I did not believe one word of them," she continued, "and now I know that some things I have read are true.

"It needed just this, perhaps, to open my eyes. Nothing of an ordinary nature would have done it. Then I came to the Fulton Street Prayer Meeting. I hardly know how I came here; but I have been here two or three times before to-day. I have seen such a difference between this and my own Church. Such prayers as these I never heard. Such remarks as these I never heard. Any one can see that they come from the heart. These two religions are so opposed to each other that only one can be true. The question has come up to my own mind—Which of these is true? And my heart answers, that what I see here in Fulton Street cannot be wrong, cannot be false. I am constrained to see that I have been deluded all my days. Now I desire to come to the truth. My husband used to pray that my heart might be enlightened. Then I did not want it. Now I do."

Some effort was made to direct her mind to Christ. She was asked if she could read the Bible?

"'Yes, I can read; but I cannot understand.'

"'You must ask to be taught of God.'

"'I know it,' said she, despondingly, 'I know it; but I do not seem to know anything about religion. I do not know *what* to do, nor *how* to do anything as I ought. I get the most light when I come to these meetings.'

"'But you must not rely on these meetings; you must rely on Christ.'

"I know it. We Catholics believe that. But I want to know how to rely on Him. That is just what I do not yet understand.'

"So," said the speaker, "I wish to ask you to pray for this poor woman, that she may be taught of God what it is to be justified by faith in Christ. The gentleman, looking over the room, said: "I do not know that she is here. I do not see her, but I hope some one will pray for her, leading this assembly in prayer."

Just as the prayer was commencing, in which her case was distinctly alluded to, she was seen entering the door-way, but on account of the crowd was unable to get in; but she kneeled down by a chair, and remained kneeling through the prayer.

The lady gave afterward good evidence that she had been the subject of renewing grace.

A man apparently near upon middle life was on his feet. He appeared to be a cultivated, educated man. He began by saying:

"I have been all my life a Roman Catholic. My father and mother were the same before me. I have travelled much, and enjoyed all that money could buy. I have never been happy. I have been coming to this prayer-meeting nearly every day for three months. It did not take me long, in the light of this meeting, to see that all the past was a sham. I never heard such prayers and experiences as I have heard in this room. I resolved to pray for the same grace. No one said anything to me, and I said nothing to others. I acted for myself on the best judgment I could form. I felt that only God could bring me out of darkness into His marvellous light. I prayed for this divine illumination. As soon as I began thus to pray, my former belief vanished away; I was no longer a poor, benighted Roman Catholic; neither was I an infidel—as I really had been, more than a Roman Catholic. It is so with many of us. We know enough to know that there is no religion in the senseless mummeries of Roman Catholic worship, and so we reject secretly all religion, because we believe there is none in this which we are taught is the only true.

"When I came here I saw that here was truth. It could be no error. And if true—these experiences, these prayers, this worship—then here I could find the way of salvation. I felt in my own soul that I was forever lost, unless God for Christ's sake would pardon my sins. I look to Jesus as the true and only Potentate, the King of kings and Lord of lords—as the only High Priest, whose mediation and intercession could avail for me.

"Oh! I cannot tell you how thankful I am in the belief and assurance that His precious blood avails for me. Jesus is exalted to be a Prince and a Saviour for me. My heart is full of praise to Him—the Chief among ten thousand."

THE DYING GIRL. 287

A Baptist minister said in distributing tracts he had encountered some cases of great interest. Then he read from a tract which he had been distributing, to show the faith in Jesus of a little dying Irish girl. Small portions of the Bible were read to her, especially the promises of Christ to a poor sinner, who longed for salvation through Him. And her mind and heart became illuminated with the heavenly spirit working within. The narrative goes on to say:

"It was about three months after Nelly had so sorely regretted his absence that Father Reilly once more stood by her bedside. After making various inquiries, and stating how it had been that he was so long away, he proceeded to say that he was now come to receive her confession and to give his absolution."

" ' I have confesssed, your reverence.'

" ' You have confessed ? ' replied the priest; ' I did not know any priest had been here except to say mass on Sundays. To whom have you confessed.'

" ' To the Lord Jesus, your reverence.'

" The priest seemed to think her mind was wandering, and said:

" ' You don't seem very well, Nelly; I'll come in the morning, and you can confess then.'

" ' I am much obliged to you, your reverence, but I'd rather not,' answered the invalid.

" ' Rather not !' repeated he, in a tone of amazement; ' do you say you'll rather not confess and get pardon of your sins as the Church commands you? Will you peril your soul in the fires of purgatory? Oh! Ellen Sullivan, I little thought this of you! Where have you learned such wicked heresy?'

"'Sure, your reverence, it is not heresy at all; and haven't I learned it all out of the Book, then, and hasn't my blessed Miss Mary been reading to me for the past three weeks every day. Oh! it is a beautiful book, the Bible, your reverence. But never a word does it say about purgatory, or yet confession—only to the great God himself through the Lord Jesus,' answered Nelly, looking devoutly up to heaven.

"The priest stood like one transfixed; but soon collecting his ideas, he said in a soft voice:

"'My poor girl, you little know the sin you have been committing; it is all a snare of the wicked one to get your soul to himself. Every one who reads the Bible, such as the heretics have, or hears it read, must be lost forever. But the Church is merciful. You did it in ignorance; so if you only confess to me as you used to do, I'll give you absolution, and you'll be all right again.'

"'I don't believe it,' said Nelly; 'indeed I don't. I would have believed it once, but now there somehow seems a great light all over me, and I can't believe it for sure how can it be wicked to read God's own book that He has written on purpose for us. And oh! Father Reilly,' added she, raising herself up and speaking with great animation, 'if you would but read it, and preach it to the poor people instead of the Latin prayers and masses they don't understand, and tell them all the sweet words it says—and how the blessed Lord Jesus sits at the right hand of the Father to hear their prayers, and not the Virgin Mary, nor the saints, oh, I know they would come to Him and be happy, just as I have done.'"

CHAPTER XVIII.

HOPE FOR THE INTEMPERATE.

In one of the meetings a man arose and said: "I beg the meeting to pray for my soul, which is in danger of being lost." Very earnest prayer followed this utterance, for the very countenance of the man bore the marks of his inward distress. As soon as the meeting was concluded, the writer sought to know more of this man's state of mind by inducing him to speak freely of his own feelings.

"Oh!" said he, "I am one of the greatest of sinners; you don't know how great a sinner I am!"

"Not so great but that you may be saved by the great Saviour."

"I know it," said he, "I know Jesus Christ can save me; and I have been coming here for two months hoping that I might find Him."

"My dear friend," we replied, "you are on the wrong tack," for we soon found out that he was the first officer of a ship. "Steer straight for Jesus, take Him on board and give Him command, and He will bring you to the desired haven."

Fifty-two requests were read in one day, and fully one-third of them were for intemperate persons, from heart-broken wives and mothers, who say that, as to worldly happiness, their lives have been miserable failures. But the case of the drunkard is not entirely hopeless. There are some in the meeting every day who not long ago were drunkards. They were men of some standing and some means, but drank to excess, and were going down to the chambers of eternal death. Now they are sober, respectably-appearing men, and often speak and pray in the meeting, and give abundant evidence that they have passed from death unto life.

THE TRUE TEMPERANCE REFORM.

Said a speaker:

"I am seventy years, old and for twenty years I was a drunkard; but my mother never gave me up. She prayed and prayed. Oh! have sympathy for the poor inebriate, and keep on praying. I know what all these requests which come from the mothers of drunken sons mean. They mean an agony of distress. How they come every day. Recently I hope I was converted."

Another said:

"The man who has never formed this terrible appetite for strong drink knows nothing of its insatiable, terrible power. If anybody is to be pitied, it is the poor drunkard. I know all about it. I have been through it all. It is the most awful bondage a man can be in. There is a fascination about the wine-cup such as you who have not come under its power can have no conception of. And I will tell you another thing—there is no cure for this but the grace of God in Jesus Christ. I do not believe in reform. I know it means nothing more than this, that a man will stand till the next temptation comes. But there are some temptations which a man cannot stand. By the grace of God, he must have the appetite obliterated, and taken entirely away. This can be done by a change of heart, such as the Holy Spirit works out in a man. Nothing else will do it. That heart must be cleansed by the blood which can cleanse from all sin. The appetite for strong drink must be eradicated. It can be, it must be! Mothers—you who pray for your sons—pray that they may be truly converted, and rest in nothing else but conversion. I tell you—for I know by my own experience—this drunkenness must be laid at the foot of the cross, and for Jesus' sake, the thirst for drink must be quenched.

"I know a woman who for thirty years walked seven miles nearly every Sabbath to church. She had a husband who had horses standing idle in the stable, but he was a drunkard. During all those years she ceased not to pray for that husband, and God heard and answered, and converted that ungodly husband, and in his last years he lived a Christian life. She went to the healing fountain for a radical cure, the change of heart bringing with it the loss of the appetite. Here we have a striking example of God's grace, of His readiness to help those who go to Him in faith."

A third speaker related the following incident: Two weeks ago he requested prayer for an intemperate family. The following Sabbath evening he spent two hours with them, and persuaded them to give up the intoxicating cup and sign the pledge of total abstinence. Last Sabbath he had the satisfaction of seeing the mother of the family standing up in a Brooklyn mission church and making public profession of her faith in Christ.

A young man said he was a clerk in this city in 1857—the year of the Great Revival. His employer persuaded him to go to the Fulton Street meeting. He was brought under the power of the Spirit at once, and soon became a Christian. Now he lives in a Western city. God has given him influence and a heart to work for Jesus, and in this work he has had great success in winning souls to Christ.

A minister said:

"I have thought I ought to say something about these drunkards to encourage their praying wives and mothers. At the time of the great revival in Ireland, following the great revival here, I paid a visit to Colerain. Among the numbers who were smitten under conviction of sin were many drunkards, and after what I have seen of their conversions, I shall never despair of the drunkards. I want to mention one case. He was not only a drunkard, but was one of the worst I ever knew of. He had been notorious in his abuse of his family. This man became one of the most devoted Christians I ever saw. I asked him to take me to his family, and as we went along—'There,' said he, pointing down the street, 'is where I killed a man, but by a mere chance I was acquitted on the trial, because they could not bring the act and prove it on me.' I never saw a more happy family or a more devoted Christian, and he declared to me that the moment Jesus was revealed to his heart the hope of glory, all his old appetite left him, and has never returned. He believed there was hope for the drunkard, if we have faith to pray for him."

Many strangers come in. Often they take part in the exercises, to the great edification of all present. On one occasion, after reading the requests, among which were many for intemperate persons, a tall, well-made, fine-looking man arose to pray, whose voice we had never heard before. He poured out his heart in fervent supplications for the drunkards whose cases had been presented, and in which he felt an interes, not easily to be accounted for. In his prayer he besought that these poor drunkards might be led to know that there was no possibility of their standing unless they stood in the strength of the Lord Jesus. No one would have known from his prayer that he was a reformed drunkard. When his prayer was over, the old missionary, sitting near, leaned over and whispered:

"That man was literally taken out of the gutter, He has been carried in out of the street many a time, where he had fallen perfectly helpless. Now you see what he is—not only a reformed man, but a thorough Christian, and knows what he prays for—that he may stand in the strength of Christ."

These words were quickly whispered while a few verses of a hymn were being read. The prayer had been tender and touching, and had moved many hearts.

Said the leader of the meeting, an eminent Christian layman:

"The great want of the church now is personal effort. I belong to a mission, which a few of us have established. A few evenings ago, when we were assembled, I saw two men looking in at the door. I beckoned to them to come in, and they drew back. I hurried to the door and invited them to come in. I saw in a moment that they had been drinking, though not to excess. I told them we took pledges to total abstinence from all intoxicating liquors. I asked them to come in and sign the pledge. One said: 'I know that drinking is a base, ruinous, sinful habit; I will sign the pledge.' And he did sign on the spot before all present.

"The other said: 'I am ready to sign the pledge; but let me go home and sign it in the presence of my wife.' And to this we all agreed. He was a manly man—full of smartness—in a good business, standing high in the community, wealthy, and if I were to name him, many of you would know him. When our meeting was concluded, I went to his home, which I found in Hudson Street. I was ushered into the parlor; all betokened ease and comfort. He called his wife and family together, and told them what he was going to do: 'I am going here, in your presence, to sign the temperance pledge, and I am going to keep it.' He then stood with uplifted hand, as if taking an oath—but it was a prayer. With his right arm uplifted, and his face set toward heaven, he said: 'I sign this pledge of total abstinence from all intoxicating drinks, and I ask God to help me keep this vow.'

"He then bent down and sign his name to the pledge. Nor was this the end. We invited him now to enlist in the service of Christ, and commit his soul into His everlasting keeping.

"The next night we had a prayer-meeting in that same parlor—a good meeting it was too; and to-night we go there again for the same purpose. And the end is not yet. We find that noble, manly man is now anxious about his soul, and we intend to follow him up till he is fully enlisted in the cause of our Divine Master.

"Thus I have illustrated what I mean by personal effort. We must seize opportunities to persuade sinners to repentance and faith in Christ, and there is no telling how much we may do if we try."

MOTHERS WILL NEVER STOP PRAYING.

Many requests come from mothers in behalf of intemperate sons, which are enough to melt the hardest heart. Said one, on rising to pray:

"O Lord! these mothers will never stop praying for the most hopeless of their intemperate sons. They will never give them up. They will never believe Thou art not able and willing to save, and when all faith fails in human help, their faith in Thee never fails. Oh! hear these poor, anxious mothers' prayers for their lost, intemperate sons, and save them with a great salvation."

The prayer was remarkable throughout—made by one whom we had never seen in the meeting before. The meeting is filling up with strangers and Western merchants who are coming into the city. They drop their business for one precious hour, and spend it here in prayer. They take the spirit of the meeting away with them, and with it warm up their prayer-meetings at home. So this meeting repeats itself all over the world.

Said one:

"I am as a brand plucked out of the burning, when I was all on fire, and almost consumed. I am thirty-six years old, and was for thirty years a miserable drunkard. I learned to drink by going after strong drink for my father, when I was only six years old. I had been a drunkard ever since, and never saw one sober day in all that time, till about eight months ago. I was picked up in the streets half intoxicated at

13*

the time, and brought into this very meeting. Here I signed the temperance pledge. I continued to come from day to day, and here I was awakened, convicted and converted. Here I had a new song put into my mouth, even praise to our God, and I hope to sing the everlasting song in heaven. Oh! what a blessed change there is in me, in my circumstances, my enjoyments, in my hopes, in my objects in life, in my family, in everything. I was poor, miserable, degraded—my family the same; when I was converted, my family had nothing to eat in the house. Before I went home I found a secret place to pray, and I knelt down and prayed fervently that God would supply us with bread somehow, or open up some way by which I could get it. When I went home I found a barrel of flour standing on my door-step. My wife said to me: 'The carman who brought this flour said it is for you.' 'Oh, no,' said I, 'it is not for me; it is a mistake, it is for some one else.' 'Yes, it is for you, he was very positive that I should tell you so.'

"I had never dreamed of praying for a barrel of flour; I did not dare to ask for so much, I could not remember when I had had a barrel of flour in my house. I have inquired of all my acquaintances, and all my friends that I met, about that barrel of flour, and I never could find out where it came from, nor the carman who brought it. Now what a happy man I am. The desire for strong drink is gone, I declare to you it is all gone. I have all I can do, and I am happy all the day long. I stand up for Jesus everywhere; I am not tongue-tied, but I speak of the love of Christ in all these streets. I am so happy; I never expected to see such a day as this; I recommend my Saviour to all I can; I never fail."

This speaker spoke very rapidly, and with great energy and deep emotion.

Another said:

"What reason I have to bless God for this prayer-meeting! I live thirty miles away in the country. I was in the habit of coming into Boston to spend my Sabbaths, and one time when I came in to have a real carouse, as was my intention, I found two of my old friends converted; and when I met them they did not hide their light under a bushel, but they talked with me—they prayed with me—and brought me here. And here the Lord met me, and had mercy on my soul. Now as often as I can get to the city, I come to this place of prayer; I am never so happy as when I can get into this room, where God had mercy on me, and spoke peace to my soul. This is the spot above all others which I shall remember longest."

It would almost seem that we are fast becoming a nation of drunkards. But it is not so, though temperance movements are in a great measure suspended, and need to be revived. Every one should endeavor to save one. Personal effort is needed to save our young men from going down to drunkards' graves. Some women ask for prayer, acknowledging that nothing but the grace of God can save them. One wife, the mother of several children, lately wrote her own most urgent request for prayer, bewailing in piteous language her enslavement to the pernicious and dreadful power of strong drink. It was prescribed for her by a physician when down with disease, and when she got up she could not forego her drink; and now she acknowledges that she has become a drunkard. She says she cannot leave it off. She is ashamed. She begs God to help her, and says unless He does she is lost forever. She has lost all confidence in her power of resistance. She has no earthly hope. She has struggled vainly, contending with this destroying curse. Her nerves are all shattered, and she is the merest wreck of her former self. Poor woman! God help her!

A VOICE FROM BOSTON.

A gentleman spoke of his coming from Boston to the Fulton Street Prayer Meeting. He said:

"I arrived this morning. As I was passing along Pearl Street, a man asked me if I would go to the noon prayer-meeting. 'Oh!' I answered, 'I shall go to the prayer-meeting.'"

So he came along, and he was glad to get up and testify to what the Lord is doing in Boston. They had precious prayer-meetings there, in the Globe Hall, at

North Street, and old South Chapel. Globe Hall is taken possession of for Christ, and the dancing and carousing are turned out. The Lord blesses the prayer meetings. The Lord hears and answers prayer. Converts are flocking to Zion with joy.

He spoke of one case of conversion. It was that of a young man. When he had found Christ for himself, he went immediately to work for others, with earnest endeavors to win them to the Saviour. Among his endeavors was one to win a poor inebriate to Christ. He found him in Boston, and he was told how wretched he was, by the poor man himself: "You do not know how miserable is my condition. While I am here, my wife and children are starving." He told him he would go and see his wife and children, if he would tell him where he lived. So he told him that he lived in Charlestown. And he went and saw them. He found a wife and three children in the most abject poverty. He found that this same poor drunkard had been once a prominent politician. He had been on the same platform, and before the same audiences as Governor B—— and the prominent men of the day—naming several as his former acquaintances and friends. The poor drunkard not only forsook his cups, but he came at once to Christ, under the influence of this young man. Then he began to work for the relief of his family, and the bettering of his temporal as well as spiritual condition. So he went to the man's former friends and inquired:

"Do you know such a man?"—naming him; and addressing Governor B., one day, soliciting aid for him.

"Oh yes! I know him. He was once a man of fair standing, but is now a great drunkard. I cannot give to him."

"But he has signed the pledge, and promised to drink no more; and, more than all, he loves the Saviour."

"Do you love the Lord Jesus Christ?"

"Yes! I love Him, and this poor man loves Him also."

Then the Governor's hand went into his pocket, and brought out some money.

"Here, this is for him?" said he.

Then he went to another and another in the same way, in every case professing for himself the same love of Christ, and pleading for his friend, because he loved Christ. Thus he unlocked the hearts of his fellow men, by his earnestness and honesty.

"Thus," said the speaker, "all may do." And he mentioned the case, he said, to show how easy is the access to all hearts.

A gentleman arose who was in middle life. His face looked as if he had fought many a hard battle with the "Apollyon"—rum. He said:

"Two years ago my friends were ashamed of me because I bore their name. They despaired of my reformation. But I found out the power Jesus has to save a man from all his enemies—even to the bitterest of all—intemperance. I went to Him for help when all had cast me off. I was reduced to nothing when I applied to Him. It was one day as I was working in the field, to earn something to keep myself from starving. It was not a long parley that we had to come to agreement. I cast myself on Him with the simple prayer—'Save, Lord—I perish!' He did save, and what a happy two years I have had with him!"

SAD, BREAKING HEARTS.

These are betrayed in such requests as follows:

"The prayer of the righteous availeth much. Pray without ceasing, that the sin of intemperance may be forsaken, and that a husband, a professing Christian, may forsake the error of his way, ere it be too late. This is the prayer of   A WIFE."

Another says:

"Will you pray for the conversion of my brother who is addicted to intemperance?   A SISTER."

Another lifts up the cry:

"Oh! do pray earnestly for my family, all of whom are going down to drunkards' graves. My heart—Oh! my heart is broken.
      "A WIFE AND MOTHER."

The following notes of thanksgiving were read at the meeting:

"A few weeks ago I asked you to pray for the conversion of my husband and two children. All have been converted. Give God all the praise." Also: "We asked your prayers that we might be blessed of the Spirit in the school-house prayer-meeting. Now, thanks be to God, we have seen His power displayed there in the hopeful conversion of ten, and more are anxious to find the Saviour." Also this: "Edinboro, February 6, 1872. Our prayers are being answered, and scores are turning to the Lord. Nearly one hundred have expressed a desire to love Jesus, and many have been hopefully converted. Pray for us, that the good work may continue."

The following communication was sent in:

"Dear Christian Brethren: I am a young business man. I have been what they call successful, but God has seen fit to check me in my eager pursuit of wealth. I am a professor of religion, and have robbed God and my own soul, and I feel that this world and its business is costing me too dear. Pray for me that I may learn the lesson that godliness with contentment is great gain, and be satisfied with what God sees fit to give.

"Yours, as I humbly trust, in Christ."

A TOUCHING CASE.

A mother, eighty-two years old, came to pray "with the dear brethren" for her son, the only child she has left out of heaven. This son she said was the father of six children. They were all exceedingly kind to her, but they were not Christians. She wanted to see them brought into the fold of Christ before she went hence to be here no more. She wished especially to see her son converted, that he might bring up his children in the nurture and admonition of the Lord.

Said a speaker.

"I propose to tell you, how the appetite for strong drink in my case was chained. A few years ago, a friend said to me: 'If you would give up smoking and drinking, you would add ten years to your life.' The habit of smoking and drinking had been formed; but I said to myself, with no little enthusiasm, 'No more drinking and smoking. Away you go!' And I thought I had done the business, and dismissed this troublesome appetite in a very summary manner. To my astonishment back again came the same appetites for smoking and drinking stronger than ever. What was I to do? *Do?* I said to myself, alarmed at my case. Do? Something must be done. If I have got where my own will is no will at all, something must be done at once. At last I prayed that God would take the accursed appetite from me. And He did. From that hour I have had no desire for strong drink."

That brief statement called up another man, who said: "For fifteen years I was a minister of the Gospel; but the appetite for strong drink would overpower me. I could not resist it. Resolution after resolution was made and broken. Finally, I said to my wife, 'Unless God interposes, I am gone!' Together we knelt, and asked our heavenly Father to take from me the fearful appetite for strong drink. From that hour of our cry, in our distress and despair, I have never had a desire to taste strong drink again."

Said another:

"An aged mother, who has asked your prayers for her son, who was led astray by wicked men, desires to return thanks to God, that He has heard your prayers in His great mercy, and has shown him the true character of those who sought his ruin. Dear friends of Christ, will you pray once more that he may be fully delivered from their power, for Jesus' sake?"

Another writes as follows:

"Reading from week to week the interesting accounts given of your meeting, and the wonderful answers to prayer, I have on several occasions asked the prayers of your meeting for the conversion of my dear husband. Four months ago this dear one was fast going the downward road of intemperance. I sent a request asking your earnest prayers in his behalf that God would give him strength to overcome his fearful appetite for intoxicating liquor. I believe that my request reached you, and believe that God heard and answered your prayers and mine. God has wonderfully kept him, in the midst of great temptations. I would desire to offer grateful praise to Almighty God. I ask your prayers that God may continue to keep him, to give him restoring grace. He is in the midst of temptation. Pray for his conversion."

"*To the Fulton Street Prayer Meeting:*

"I yesterday arose with difficulty in the meeting, to request your prayers in my behalf, that I may be enabled to refrain entirely from intoxicating drink. I believe the Almighty God has answered you, for His Son Jesus' Christ sake. I am in my fiftieth year, and in nineteen years that I have been in this country, I have been engaged no fewer than twenty-seven times, in eighteen mercantile houses in this city, and have been discharged from each engagement, with the exception of only two, for intemperance. One house engaged me four times, two houses, three times each the rest twice and once—all situations of trust and responsibility. The two exceptions were where old employers, seeing me steady, offered me inducements to come back to them. Some situations I have held between one and two years. Others I have not been able to hold on to more than one week. Born of pious parents, who, I believe, are now in heaven; sent early to Sabbath-school as a scholar, and going afterward as a teacher many years, how amazing is God's long-suffering mercy to me, that He has permitted me to pollute the earth so long, and provide for me so many means of support! From the age of twenty-two years, intemperance began to grow upon me. I lost my situations in Liverpool in consequence of it; was in business on my own account, and failed through it, before coming to the United States. Oh, my brethren! I can never describe how thankful I am; cannot thank the Lord sufficiently for His mercy in opening my eyes to the heinousness of my offences. I got so far that the devil began comparing in my brain the easiest modes of suicide."

Another writes, saying:

"Beloved Friends in Christ: I recently sent you a special plea for prayer for a dear friend, who, I felt, was careless and indifferent in regard to spiritual things and Christian duties, and who seemed to be on the very verge of ruin by intemperance. I write now to tell you, with a heart filled with faith and gratitude, that our blessed prayer-hearing God has already given us an earnest—a token of His willingness to hear and fulfil our petitions, and give us the good gifts we ask for this precious soul. Oh, will you not continue to pray for him—to help the helpless? Oh, let us put God in remembrance. Let us plead together. Pray that he who is exposed daily to many temptations, and who has no strength in himself to resist them, may have abundant supplies of overcoming grace and strength given him from on high. I feel my heart burn within me, as I appeal for an interest in your prayers, and a sweet assurance that God will give His Holy Spirit in answer."

A young man arose and said he had come into the meeting to ask us to pray for a rumseller, who had resolved to quit the unholy traffic of supplying "distilled damnation" to men to drink, and thus drown them in perdition. A clergyman arose and engaged in prayer, thanking God that in His providence many eyes and hearts are opening to the enormity of the sin of intemperance and the flood of ruin which is sweeping over the land, bearing away thousands of our young men to drunkards' graves. He prayed that a divine hand might avert the evils that are coming upon us as a nation, and that God would move His people to withstand them by every means in their power. His prayer was very fervent, and many were the low but heartfelt amens when it was concluded.

CHAPTER XX.

GROWTH IN GRACE.

THESE meetings have been the means of aiding many Christians to the enjoyment of richer spiritual experience than they had ever had before. One day a Presbyterian Christian said:

"We hear a great deal said about the higher Christain life. For my part, I don't know anything about it. I only know it becomes me to be very humble, and to cry out every day, 'God be merciful to me, a sinner.'"

He resumed his seat, and a Baptist minister arose and summed up the matter by saying:

"All I know of the higher Christian life is to let the promises and assurances of the Gospel get full possession of the heart. It is but a short step from the orthodoxy of the head to the orthodoxy of the heart. That step I trust I have taken. I have accepted full and complete salvation on the terms of the Gospel. As for my sins, God knows I have repented of them, and according to His promise He has removed them from me as far as the east is from the west; and as for my transgressions, I shall see them no more forever, for God has said it. And if I sin, I go to my advocate with the Father, and ask for renewed forgiveness, and I get it. I do not have to ask for it over and over again, and have the same act of mercy bestowed a hundred times for the same offences. No! no! I take God at His word. I believe every word He says, and believing, I rejoice. It was not always so with me. I had very narrow and inadequate views of the Gospel. I did not half believe it. I did not half receive it, though I supposed I did. I had no idea of how I came short. The old notion was, that God did a little yesterday, and a little to-day, and would do a little to-morrow, and so on through life, and at last the blessed work of salvation would be completed, and I should enter heaven. Thank God! this meeting has taught me that if I truly believe on Christ, for His sake I am saved with an everlasting salvation.

"I have not to wait till I draw my last breath in the dissolution of the body, to be saved. But I am saved the moment I believe. But we do not accept it as an experience. Do you want an inspired witness to this matter of experience? Let us call one. Saint Paul says: 'I know on whom I have believed, and am persuaded that He is able to keep that which I have committed to Him, against that day. There is no condemnation to them who are in Christ Jesus—who are kept by the power of God through faith unto salvation.' Now if this is true, why should I not tell it to assure sinners what a wonderful redemption is prepared for them? I must tell this not only as a doctrine, but as an experience—tell it every day to poor perishing souls, as the glorious Gospel of the blessed God. This giving all to Jesus, desiring all from Jesus, and having all in Jesus, is all the higher Christian life I know.

> "'I lay my sins on Jesus,
> The spotless Lamb of God,
> He takes them all and frees us
> From the accursed load.'"

In a moment a young man was seen standing in the back part of the room. He was brushing away the tears. He was pale and sickly in appearance. As soon as he could, he said:

"Mr. Chairman—It is only a few weeks since I sent you a request that this meeting pray for my conversion. God almost at once answered your prayers, and I can say I have had the happy experience which has just been described. When my salvation came, it was as a river, and my peace was an overflowing stream. I accepted Christ for all He is offered—my wisdom, righteousness, sanctification, and redemption. I had been a great sinner. But what a Saviour I found Him!—so unspeakably precious."

A clergyman said:

"There is much said nowadays about the higher life. All the higher life I know anything about is taking hold on Christ with a stronger faith, and making more of his offices and work. I do not think I ever knew Christ to be so exalted in this meeting as now. I think I can see a great advance in the faith and spirit of consecration among these brethren and sisters who come. I do not hear them say that they live sinless lives. But I do hear them say that Jesus saves to the uttermost, and that the blood of Jesus Christ cleanses from all sin. I believe it with all my heart. I have no doubts about it. I have full assurance of these mighty truths. They have gained possession of my soul, and my heart is full of joy unspeakable. I confess to you that I am one of the happiest of men. It is not a new doctrine. It is as old as the Bible. But it is a new experience. I might have had it before, but I did not. I did not have in my own soul a realization of the truth as I now have. I can sing all day long—

> "'There is a fountain filled with blood,
> Drawn from Immanuel's veins;
> And sinners plunged beneath that flood.
> Lose all their guilty stains.'

"This is the same old-fashioned theology that Paul believed when he said, 'I know in whom I have believed.' There is nothing new about it. It is all as old as the Bible. It is suited to our wants. We want just such a Gospel. This is the higher Christian life, to walk by the faith of the Son of God. There is joy in thus knowing Jesus. Let us tell it to sinners all around."

SHALL NOT WANT ANY GOOD THING.

Another remarked:

"I needed just that passage, and God by His Spirit

helped me to believe in His faithfulness to fulfil His own word. On that text, as on a hinge, my heart turned to seek the Lord, and I gave up cheerfully all my fancied wealth for the sake of a saving interest in the Lord Jesus Christ. The load of guilt was gone, and I felt that I had salvation through the blood of the Lamb. The struggle was over, and my peace flowed as a river.

"Some unconverted, awakened sinner, here may ask me, 'How about that promise?' I will answer. When my heart began to trust God I forgot all about the promise. I had all my heart desired in Jesus Christ. But God did not forget *that* promise, though I did; and I can truly say from that moment when I first believed Him, I have never been in want of *any* good thing. I found that He remembered to give me what I did not expect to ask, and in His abundant mercy he has always kept His word to the very letter. Of this world's goods I have had all I could have asked, and even more. But best of all, *I have been made alive unto Christ forever more.* I am going home to die no more. For me it is not *death* to die. I thank God for that 34th Psalm; it led me to trust God through Jesus Christ. 'They that *seek* the Lord shall not want any good thing.'

> "Oh make but trial of His love,
> Experience will decide
> How blest are they, and only they,
> Who in His love confide."

An elderly gentleman arose. He said that his experience of the grace of God had been much varied in the different parts of his life. Formerly he had been possessed of large means. Now he was not worth ten dollars in the world. For thirty years he professed religion, and, as he supposed, lived a very regular and exemplary life. But it was not a life of faith in the Son of God. He added:

"I have no doubt that all those thirty years I was a Christian. Sometimes I was doubting—sometimes hoping with more confidence. But much of the time I was fearing. I was in bondage to sin all those thirty years. I knew little of the grace of God. After all those thirty years of what the world called consistent Christian living, it was wonderful how little life I had, and it was still more wonderful that I should be brought to that grace in which I now hope I stand, and should be freed from that spirit of bondage and fear, and should be brought by Divine grace into full assurance of faith. I have no fear. I have that peace which no language can describe. I never knew until lately that there was such meaning in that language of the Apostle in the 6th chapter of Romans: 'But now being made free from sin, and become servants to God, ye have your fruit unto holiness and the end everlasting life!' I never believed Christ for this. I did not know what it was to feel *assured* that the blood of Jesus Christ cleanseth from all sin. I knew that Christ was able to save such a sinner as I. But I never, in all those thirty years, felt that I was saved. I hoped to be saved, but felt that after all I might be a castaway. But now how different it is with me. I feel that I have committed all to God, and that I am saved through the blood of Jesus Christ."

REST IN FAITH.

A Presbyterian minister said he had been in the meeting a few times lately, and on one occasion he was greatly edified with the remarks which he had heard in respect to the rest which the Christian might enjoy if he would fully trust in the Lord Jesus Christ. Said he:

"There is a rest which is a matter of experience, and there is a rest which is a matter of inheritance. One belongs to time, the other to eternity; one to earth, the other to heaven. It is a noticeable fact that many requests which come here are from timid, anxious, doubting Christians. They are afraid to trust Christ. They do not feel assured that the work is all accomplished for their salvation. Now why not so believe as to trust your immortal souls to His care and keeping now and forever? He is the author of our faith, the end of our faith, and He has declared He will be the finisher of our faith; and He who has begun the good work in us, will carry it to the day of perfect and everlasting redemption. Why not take hold of Christ in the largest, fullest sense by faith, and let this rest, which is a matter of present experience, be yours to enjoy? Be comforted, that you may trust Jesus in a measure so full that you may rejoice in Him at all times with exceeding joy—joy unspeakable, and full of glory.

"Think how much reason you have to trust Him. What has He not done to inspire your trust in Him? He bore your sins in His own body on the tree. He carried your sorrows. He was wounded for your transgressions, and bruised for your iniquities, and by His stripes you are healed. He has made full and perfect satisfaction to the claims of a violated law, so that, being in Christ Jesus, there is no condemnation; you are justified, you are sanctified through the shedding of His blood, and soon you will be glorified together with Him.

"Accept then the salvation which He has wrought out for you. It cannot be made more complete than He has made it. On the Redeemer's work and righteousness you may build your hopes, full of assurance and joy. Thus the rest which is by faith in the Son of God will be yours—*rest* which is a matter of blessed and happy experience, will be yours. And this rest is a sweet foretaste of that rest which remaineth for the people of God, which shall be your eternal inheritance."

The minister did not say a word about himself or his own experience; but every one who heard him felt that he knew what he was talking about—that the faith in Jesus he exhorted others to have he had in lively exercise in his own soul.

There were many followed him, who gave delightful testimony of this grace, wherein they stand with full assurance of faith and hope. It was said we ought not so to dishonor Christ as not trust Him. We have no right to doubt—to go with our heads bowed down as bulrushes, as if it was dangerous to hope, and we have an immovable foundation to build our hopes upon; and he that buildeth thereon shall never be put to confusion. Why not hope with assurance?

HIGHER SPIRITUAL LIFE.

Said a speaker:

"If this world is ever converted, it must be by the power of a higher Christianity. We must have a higher spiritual life. It has been said by a distinguished clergyman that *the church is dying of respectability.* Oh! it is so respectable to be in the fashion—to have splendid equipages—to be handsomely dressed—to live above all possible comfort in the effort to live a little better—dress a little more extravagantly, to appear to be wealthy—to live like beggars within door, and to appear like princes without. Our pious women, or women professing godliness, carry on their backs the hard earnings of their husbands and fathers—and while they are flaunting their gay dresses and airing their vanity, their male friends are studying to know how they shall save themselves from bankruptcy. O! it is pitiful to see how the good old ways are being forsaken, when families professing godliness were an example to the world.

"We most come back to the simplicity of an earnest Christian life, or the world can never be converted.

And it is astonishing how much we may do when we follow Christ and are filled with His spirit. I have had an opportunity to know something of the power of a single man, when imbued with the spirit of entire consecration to Jesus. I can tell the name of a young man who has been the means of the conversion of more than 800 young men, whose salvation can be traced directly to him. His influence is felt and acknowledged. The city in which he lives was once a very Sodom, and now it is one of the safest and most moral cities in the land. And the moral transformation has been brought about by the influence of a single young man! And what is the secret of his influence? Why it is this, that he has given himself to the work of following the Lord fully. He seeks to do—not his own will, but the will of his divine Lord. He is determined to do by the day all he can for Jesus.

"Now what hinders all from doing and living the same glorious life and doing the same thing? What hinders a thousand young men from the same spirit of consecration? Suppose a thousand young men in any of our great cities—rather in all of them—were living as does the young man of whom I speak, who can estimate the change that would come over the nation? Why not have a thousand such workers in every State in this broad land? What mighty harvests would be gathered. Why not have the sowers and the reapers?

"What are the 50,000 professors of religion in this city doing for the conversion of the city to God? We rejoice to know that there are a great many devoted Christians in the city of New York—doing an immense amount of good. But let an influence from the highest come over them and inspire them with a spirit of entire consecration to Jesus, and what a change would come. Oh! who can estimate the world of good which might be done by these 50,000?"

SEIZING OPPORTUNITIES.

An earnest man said he believed we could not create opportunities, because he believed God gave them, and when He gives them we should seize hold on them and improve them. And in regard to them and the right improvement of them, he believed there was a mandate and a provision from God himself. Said he:

" I cannot forbear speaking on the subject of religion to persons I have never seen before, and I am encouarged to pray and believe as if I knew a gracious answer would come. I can illustrate what I mean by a recent occurrence: I was riding on the front platform of a street railroad car. I was alone with the driver. I said to myself, 'Now, shall I speak to this young man about his soul? Shall I show myself a witness for Jesus?' Something seemed to say, 'You had better not. You know you have no talent of that kind. You never had any tact in that direction. So don't worry about this young man, and make a fool of yourself. You are a perfect failure in this regard. You cannot say a sensible thing. Some men can; but you cannot. You never could. You are particularly unfortunate in this. You have no duty to do of this nature, because what you cannot do you are not required to try to do.'

"I thought I knew whose suggestions these were, and I determined to put an end to the strife at once by speaking; for another voice said, 'Speak to that young man.' I did speak to him. I found him a professor of religion, but a great backslider. He had gone far astray, and was in a very uneasy, anxious state of mind. He acknowledged his error with much emotion and apparent sorrow. I parted from him with tears in my eyes. I saw them standing in his when I bid him good-by. He grasped my hand, and begged me to pray for him. I asked him if he would go at once to the blessed Saviour, and ask him to forgive all his backslidings and blot out his iniquities, and help him henceforth to honor him by a consecrated and holy life. He said he would with the grace of God, and so we parted. I felt the power of prayer in my heart, for my heart was full of prayer, and I felt assured that my prayers would be answered. This is what I mean by a command and a promise."

Another speaker arose—a young man, twenty-five to thirty years of age. He looked pale and sickly. The meeting had just finished singing the stanza—

> "The soul that on Jesus hath leaned for repose,
> I will not, I will not, desert to his foes;
> That soul, though all hell should endeavor to shake,
> I'll never, no never, no never forsake."

The words had been sung with great fervor, and

when they were finished, there stood the young man endeavoring to seize the opportunity to speak. He said:

"I can testify to the truth of the remarks which have just been made. But a few months ago I sent a request to this meeting on my own behalf, asking you to pray for my conversion. And I humbly believe your prayers have been answered. Since then, I have been almost to the gates of the Celestial City. I got to the banks of the Jordan of death. I seemed to hear the voice of one saying, 'Fear not.' There were no turbid billows, no rolling floods—all was calm and peaceful; and if I had stepped in, I am sure the waters would have divided, and I should have gone over on dry land. But God only let me *look over* to the other side. The time had not come to *go over*.

"Since my wonderful recovery, I have been examining this 'fear not,' and I find when these words are used in the Bible, they are almost always accompanied with a promise. When thrust into the prison, it is, 'Fear not: I will be with thee;' into the water-floods, it is, 'Fear not: they shall not overflow thee;' into the flames, it is, 'Fear not: they shall not kindle upon thee.' Oh, how precious all these promises! how precious! The Gospel means a great deal to me; and it must, or *I* could have no hope. *I* need to be saved to the uttermost; for I had been to the uttermost a sinner."

LETTING GO AND TAKING HOLD.

A minister said a great many undertake to tell *how*

the sinner may believe on Christ. But they undertake to tell what never can be told. No Christian can tell it. Not an angel in heaven can explain it. We can state the facts and the experience, but that is all we can do. We can say we did not believe in Jesus once, but now we do believe. But not one of us can tell how the chasm between unbelief and belief was bridged over—or how we stepped from the one to the other. That cannot be told, for we do not know it ourselves. Faith is the gift of God; but by what methods He imparts this to the soul He has never revealed to us. The blind, restored to sight by Jesus, could not tell how it was done. All he could say was, "Whereas I was blind, now I see." So with the sinner who has been persuaded to trust in Christ. His faith has been inspired—he knows not how; all he knows is that he now believes in Jesus to the great joy of his heart. The speaker added:

"Faith is a letting go and a taking hold. We let go of the things we cling to, and we take hold on Christ, whom we never trusted before. We cannot reason about it. Faith is not subject to reason. It is above reason. Faith does not look for evidences, for then it would not be faith. Faith believes without being able to assign any reasons for it."

Another clergyman very happily illustrated this matter of letting go and taking hold—letting go of the world and taking hold on Christ. He said there were three men in partnership in business. For a time the business of the firm went on very smoothly. One of these men was a Christian, and the other two were not. After a time the business took on another shape. It did not go on in a straightforward, honest way. It was not on the square. The Christian man was greatly troubled about it. He had not neglected the souls of his partners. He had often spoken with each of them on the subject of personal religion, all to no effect. He told them how he found matters going in business. It was not conducted on Christian principles. They told him it was conducted on business principles, that BUSINESS IS BUSINESS. He was not satisfied, and made up his mind that he must leave the firm; they were making money fast, yet he was not satisfied to make it in that way. He told his partners:

"You know that I have not been remiss in my duty to you. I have tried to persuade you to become Christians. I have talked with you often. I have prayed with you constantly. I see no change and no disposition to change, and our firm must be dissolved. I cannot go against my conscience for the sake of making money. We must part company. And now do you write out the terms on which the firm shall be dissolved."

To this they agreed, and at once set about their work. Soon they began to tire of their work and said to each other, "We cannot spare this man. He is an element of power among us. We cannot do without him." And so they told him, "We have talked over this whole matter of dissolution, and we believe that you must remain."

"No," said the Christian man, "I cannot remain. I cannot satisfy my mind and heart by saying business is business, to cover up iniquity. I will not be a party to any mode of doing business which is contrary to my conscience. I assure you that sin is sin—no matter if you do call it business."

So he insisted that they should proceed to the dissolution.

Meantime these partners admitted to each other that their friend's position was right, and theirs was wrong. The more they reflected the more they felt condemned. The Holy Spirit began to deal very faithfully with them, and they saw themselves in their naked moral deformity, and finally became true Christians.

The pious member of the firm had gone through a fiery trial in making up his mind to quit his business. The more he thought, the more he saw that the world must be given up, and Christ must be received and held on to. And it was this very thing—this tenacious holding on to Christ—that was the means of leading his partners to Christ.

"THE MEMORY OF THE JUST IS BLESSED."

Elder S—— was born in Vermont, and early in life removed to Western New York. He was the son of a deacon S—— of eminent piety, and had a long line of ancestry distinguished for their devotedness to the service of the Lord Jesus. In this meeting there is sometimes a leader who bears this honored name. He comes in quietly from his railroad-office nearly every day, and joins in the services of the hour; and sometimes leads the meeting. He is a cousin to this Elder S——, previously alluded to. The story was told of a conversation he had with a young man just entering the ministry, as illustrating what a few words may do—said to the right person, at the right time, and in the right spirit.

The last years of Elder S—— were spent at St. Catharines, Canada West. A young licentiate who had supplied the Presbyterian church in that place for a few Sabbaths, tells his own story:

"The few months of preaching had been finished, and I was about leaving for Rochester. I was on my way to the railroad depot to take the cars, and was joined by the Elder, who soon finished the commonplaces of our meeting and proceeded directly to the matter that had led him to take this walk with me. Said he: 'I have had a great desire that you should aim at something more than being a minister of average piety. I shall never be satisfied to know that you consent to be ranked as a good minister, as the world would call you. There is something higher and better.'

"The Elder went on with instance and illustration, explaining and unfolding his idea of a New Testament minister, as he conceived it. There was an inspired light in his eye, an indescribable and tender unction in his tone. Partly what he said, but far more his saying it as he did, moved me inexpressibly to feel the solemn weight of his earnest words. At the close of our talk he drew from his pocket a tract. It was entitled, 'Spiritual Religion.' He gave it to me as a seal and confirmation of his views and desires in my behalf.

"During my first brief pastorate that same tract circulated from hand to hand, and the story of how it was given to me was the means of a revival of religion which continued like a long April day of sun and showers, in producing blossom and fruit in their season, till broken health brought my ministry in that place to a close. I have since longed to see more such men in our churches, to minister to the young Timothys that minister to them.

"Oh! that this meeting might be the great instrumentality for raising up such lay helpers, to be aids to those who preach the glorious Gospel of the blessed God!

"This Elder was only what all our elders may be, *and must be*, in order that the Gospel may have free course and be glorified in the salvation of souls, and the proclamation of the Gospel may be such that the preacher may both save himself and them that hear him. We must have a spiritual religion in our churches and among our laymen, as well as among pastors and elders. Oh! for more Harlan Pages! When shall we have them in all our churches and among all our people?"

CHAPTER XXI.

THE REVIVAL OF 1872.

THE early part of the year was made memorable by numerous revivals of religion in widely distant parts of the United States of America. Their relation was intimate with the Week of Prayer, and the daily prayer meetings that prolonged the week into weeks of supplication. One of the early records of the Fulton Street meeting, was in these words:

"There is an amazing interest about this meeting. It is as in days gone by: the Spirit of the Lord overshadows the assembly of God's people. The meetings are full to overflowing; but the interest is not measured by the numbers present. Awakened sinners are in the meeting every day, and the voices of those who have lately found Christ here are often heard. Many, awakened to their perishing condition, send requests from a distance for supplication in their behalf—so that the strivings of the Spirit are felt in other places as well as here. Many pastors and churches send requests to the meeting that prayer may be offered for the outpouring of the Holy Spirit upon pastor, church, and people. These are growing more numerous than they have been before for many years. Many are looking for a mighty outpouring of the Holy Spirit. Bodies of ministers who have been lately together have felt the strong persuasion that the Lord is about to open the windows of heaven and pour down such a blessing as that there shall be hardly room to receive it. There is much prayer for this, that the Lord will revive his work."

For some months the great cry of this meeting was for the outpouring of the Holy Spirit upon the churches in all lands, and upon the whole world. Indeed, this burden of supplication began far back in the year 1871. It was evident that there was a little cloud arising out of the sea, giving token that the whole heaven would be soon overcast, and the shower of divine grace was about to descend. With the approach of the Week of Prayer, we began to have notices of religious awakening in some of the churches, and special supplication was made for the outpouring of the Holy Spirit as in the time of the great revival of 1858; and the Spirit has come upon the churches, not as then. Now it is the silent and gentle rain, coming upon all the land. Then it was the mighty shower, coming down like a torrent, and sweeping all before it. The wave crossed the ocean and swept over other lands, and great was the company of those who became obedient to the faith. Then it claimed universal attention, and made subsidiary to it the power of the secular and religious press, as great instrumentalities in promoting it. The news of conquests of the Spirit went as on the wings of the wind, and was wafted to all countries, and thousands enlisted under the banner of the cross. Half a million were added to the churches in this country alone, not to speak of other lands, as the statistics of the period show.

Now a quiet work has been and is going on in the churches, and the first we know of it is the publication of the numbers who have been added to the churches on their last coummunion seasons. Requests for prayer for the Spirit come from every quarter. Some say, "Why can we not have a revival of religion in our church? Why not?"

The revival spirit has not come as in 1858, and yet God has sent it. Men prayed for just such a divine display now as then, by the same methods. God has chosen a different way to make men see that the *method* of operation was nothing; but the divine work is everything. So it is not of him that willeth, nor of him that runneth; but of God, who showeth mercy. So we are all constrained to cry, Not unto us, *not unto us*, oh Lord! but to Thy name be ALL THE GLORY! This is the substance of remarks made, following the reading of a large number of requests for prayer for the Holy Spirit. Such requests as the following were offered:

"The prayers of this meeting are earnestly desired for a pastor and congregation where God has commenced the work of the Holy Spirit. Plead with God that this work may be carried on with great power."

From a military post in Oregon:

"I come to you earnestly asking your prayers for myself and husband, and for the whole garrison. Oh, pray that the Holy Spirit may descend and rest upon us, for we sadly need His influence. Pray for our chaplain, that he may not be discouraged.

(Signed) "The Wife of an Army Officer."

A gentleman said:

"I came two hundred miles to get to this meeting. I was charged, when leaving the place where I reside, to be sure to come to this meeting. I have never been here before, and may never be again. But I want to bear my testimony to the preciousness of this place of prayer. I feel that the Holy Spirit is here. I feel awed by a sense of the Divine Presence. I am the superintendent of a Sabbath-school. It is large and flourishing, and there is some religious feeling among us. But I want you to pray that God would open a window in heaven, and pour us down such a blessing there shall be no room to receive it. God help us in prayer to-day for this."

He sat down, deeply moved. The leader asked him to lead in prayer, and in doing so he showed he had been accustomed to go to the throne of grace.

His prayer was very fervent, for all the objects which had been presented to the meeting.

A gentleman then arose and said:

"A young lady sits near me who desires that I will ask you to pray for her. She says she wants to become a Christian *to-day*, here, before she leaves this sacred place of prayer. The leader said, after singing—

> "Just as I am without one plea
> But that thy blood was shed for me,
> And that thou bidst me come to thee,
> Oh, Lamb of God, I come:"

"Will some brother pray for this young lady, and pray that she may remember that, while she thinks she is seeking Jesus, Jesus is here seeking her. Remember the parable of the woman who lost the piece of silver, seeking diligently till she found it. And of the shepherd, who lost one sheep and left the ninety and nine, going after it, and leaving all the others and looking till he finds it; and laying it on his shoulders, he comes back with it rejoicing. This is Jesus going after the lost. So Jesus comes here to-day, seeking this lost young woman, and he knocks at the door of her heart, saying, 'I am here. Behold, I stand at the door and knock; open the door, and I will come in.' Now, while we are singing, or before we sing,—now, this moment,—let this heart be opened to receive Christ."

The singing being concluded, prayer followed, by

one who seemed to realize that he stood between the living and the dead—so earnest, so importunate, were those supplications. More than one prayer followed. The meeting proceeded in the usual manner, only the leader said he had no doubt that the room was filled with anxious sinners—perhaps more of this class than any others; and the hymns he gave out to be sung were suited to such cases.

In the course of a few weeks joyful intelligence came from all parts of the country, that God is visiting His people, and that great numbers of souls are converted to the Lord. In most cases these seasons of revival dated from the Week of Prayer, now so generally observed throughout Christendom. In many churches the Week of Prayer was anticipated by the appointment of preliminary services, and when that period arrived, those who met to pray found that the Spirit was already moving upon the hearts of the people, that Christians were unusually quickened, and that many were anxiously inquiring what they must do to be saved. The connection between the prayers of God's people with their renewed consecration to His service, and the blessing, has been very marked. While they were yet calling, God had heard and answered with the abundant effusions of His grace. One feature of the revival, more marked than in any similar season of refreshing, not only characterizes it as a genuine work of the Spirit, but also inspires hope in regard to the future of the Church. It is the spirit of unity among various denominations which has preceded and accompanied these quickenings. Letters from all parts of the land brought the same intelligence, that the various evangelical denominations not only united in the observance of the Week of Prayer, but continued to pray and labor together with one accord in seeking their mutual edification, and the salvation of souls around them. There may be exceptions to this feature of the work, but this is the uniform testimony of those who sent accounts of revivals, and we hail it as another indication of the progress of that spirit which must characterize the whole Church before the world will believe that God has sent His Son to be the Saviour. It is becoming more and more evident that Christians of various surnames are sinking the minor differences that divide them, and exalting the one great name, the only name given under heaven among men whereby they can be saved, and making Christ's Church and Christ's work, and the salvation of souls more important than the building up of a mere denomination.

Specific cases of answers to prayer were frequent.

Some time ago a request was sent for prayer for the outpouring of the Holy Spirit upon a church, and this prayer had been answered in the conversion of so many that one hundred and forty-eight had been added to the Church at the last communion.

A gentleman said he had just come from attendance upon a meeting of the Presbytery of New York. He spoke of that session especially which was given up to conversation and accounts of the state of religion. He said most of the churches had some good news to report of the conversion of sinners. Many had been the seasons of refreshing from the presence of the Lord.

An old returned missionary suggested that it would be well for all Christendom to hold a year of prayer, as this meeting does, and then another year of prayer, and so on and on, till the whole world is converted. One of the hindering causes of the continuance of a revival was found in contemplating an end to it, which actually puts an end to it. A revival should have no end.

The following is an example of earnest desire and hope:

"Dear Brethren—I wrote to you, asking your earnest prayers for my husband, some time ago, and for myself and for the church in this place. Your prayers have been, in a great degree, answered. The church is beginning to be revived, and new prayer-meetings are being organized. The church seems to be more alive than ever I knew it before. No one except my husband knows that I have written to you to pray for us. They are wondering what this can mean—what the cause can be. My husband has commenced his studies, preparatory for the Gospel ministry. Oh, pray for him, that he may be endued with wisdom from on high, and that everything may be made plain to him, and that we both may be filled with the Holy Spirit, so that we may be faithful and efficient workers in the vineyard of our Lord. Oh, I beseech you that you will pray earnestly for the outpouring of the Holy Spirit, and for a glorious revival of religion here, for sin and wickedness abound. Our church are praying for and expecting a revival. We want you to unite your prayers with ours, that God will abundantly bless us."

The above comes from a Western town. The following is of a different character, and shows how wide is the range of these requests for prayer:

"Murfreesboro' Tenn.,
April 22, 1872.

"Dear Brethren—We have had no special seasons of grace in our beloved Cumberland Presbyterian Church since 1866, and we have been without a pastor since Christmas, but expect another this week. Brethren, pray for us and for our incoming pastor, that he may come filled with the Holy Ghost, and that God would revive His work once again, and that this year may be fraught with great blessings to us, and especially to myself.

"An Elder."

A letter came from Long Island, which said:

"Brethren, pray for us. This is the petition our little praying circle resolved, last night, to send you. Pray that the quickening power of the Holy Spirit may rest upon our pastors, our church membership, our Sunday-schools, our congregation, and our community generally. We are praying and laboring for a revival of religion as the surest means of reuniting a people long estranged by local church dissensions."

A request for prayer came from Maine, embracing a list of one hundred and thirty-one persons, for whom prayer was asked, that they might be converted.

A gentleman arose and said:

"I feel an interest in that town and that list of names. I was from an adjoining town, and my wife was from that very town; and having looked over this list, I find I know a good many of these people. I hope you will pray for the conversion of every one."

A clergyman told us of a blessed work of grace going on in a mission where he labored, in the upper part of this city. Prayer had been offered for the conversion of particular individuals, and they had been converted. He said he was about to open a new mission, and he desired prayer that God would grant abundant success.

On one day five churches, holding a series of meetings, sent in their requests for prayer. These petitions contained earnest appeals for supplication for backsliders.

Every day there is a call to thanksgiving. Sometimes there are many calls on the same day, reaching the meeting from different quarters. Among others, the following has been received from Iowa:

"My faith in believing prayer has been greatly strengthened by reading accounts of God's gracious answers to prayer offered at the Fulton Street Prayer Meeting. Oh that I could meet and unite with you in praising God for His wonderful works to the children of men. A few years ago, while deeply convicted of sin, I wrote a request asking an interest in your prayers. I have always believed that God heard and answered, for I soon experienced the blessedness of those whose transgressions are forgiven and whose sins are covered. Dear friends, for this let us give thanks unto the Lord."

A pastor of a church said:

"God is blessing us with the outpouring of the Holy Spirit. About seventy have been hopefully converted. Pray for us."

Some prayed for a mighty baptism from on high.

Some spoke of the great revival as already commenced. Some were animated with strong confidence and hope, and some filled with fear that the season might go by and leave no blessing. On the whole, the expressions of hope were more than the expressions of fear. One clergyman said he came to the meeting with his heart full of thanksgiving, and he asked them to join him in ascriptions of praise to our God, who had heard and answered prayer offered for him and his church. "Yesterday," said the speaker, who is the pastor, " we received thirty to the communion of the church. The work of grace is begun among us, and we ask you to pray that God will carry it on with mighty power."

A gentleman arose and said he had been in Great Britain and on the Continent for most of the time for several years, and wherever he went he found the fame of this meeting had gone before him. He continued:

"It is a power for good, not only here in New York and in this country, but throughout the world. And it is all of God that it has been made the means of so much good. It has demonstrated to the world the *power of prayer*. The reports of your meetings, which are published, are transferred to the religious papers of the old world, and are translated into other languages, and are thus scattered abroad, so that what is done and said here is not hid in a corner. These things being so, there is great responsibility resting upon this meeting, to preserve its original type, which I am happy to find it does, and keep to itself the great feature of being simply a prayer-meeting. Years ago I was here and was in the habit of attending this place of prayer. I am happy to find, on coming home and coming into this meeting, that it is the same that it was years ago. So may it continue to be in years to come—to many souls the house of God and the gate of heaven."

The speaker became very animated in his address as he insisted that simple, earnest prayer should be the distinguishing and marked feature of this meeting.

A Western man said on the last Sabbath, he, with ninety-eight others, had made public profession of their faith in Christ, in Wisconsin, and on the same day about sixty had joined another church in the same place—all as the fruits of a great and glorious revival of religion. The work was still in progress. The town had been wonderfully blessed, and the number of conversions bore a large proportion to the number of inhabitants.

Several spoke of revivals prevailing in the places of their residence, and requested prayer for the outpouring of the Holy Spirit in more copious measure. Daily meetings were being held, brought down from the Week of Prayer.

Said a clergyman:

"I love to preach Jesus—beginning, middle, and end of our salvation. And we do not half get what is provided for us, because we all lay hold of it by faith and consecration. Now, as a matter of doctrine, we all believe that our salvation is from God through Jesus Christ. We all believe in this that our all comes from Him, and our all is in Him, but when we come to believe in our all to Him, then our selfishness is at fault. We think we have many things that are really ours. No! All is the Lord's; the silver and the gold His, the cattle upon a thousand hills, His. Come now, lay all your business at the feet of Jesus. Give your all to Him, and you will prove the truth of His saying: 'Every one that hath forsaken homes, or brethren, or sisters, or father, or mother, or wife, or children, or lands, for my name's sake, shall receive an hundred-fold, and shall inherit everlasting life.'"

The speaker was a Presbyterian minister, who said he had been in great revivals in the East, but never in one of such amazing power as in the Rocky Mountains, among the miners. One of the first things they had to learn was their entire dependence upon the Holy Spirit; and another thing was that there was nothing too hard for God to do—no heart so hard that He could not subdue it. The work went on with majestic power. It was all the work of the Lord and His matchless grace. It extended to all classes. From ninety to one hundred and twenty had been hopefully converted in the Rocky Mountains, where men's hearts were as hard as the rocks. The power of the Spirit was wonderfully manifested in the conversion of the most hardened among them; and from many a miner's camp there went up the sounds of praise and prayer, and the mountains became vocal with the praises of our God. The speaker added:

"Oh, it was glorious to witness such a revival! There was one feature of the use of means which I think I ought to mention. It is this: God was exalted; God—Father, Son, and Holy Ghost—was exalted so as I never saw anywhere else, and men's hearts melted like wax before the flame."

Then came a request from Cleveland, Tennessee, under date of May 1st, 1872:

"*To the Fulton Street Prayer Meeting*:

Dear Brethren—The Ministers' and Pastors' Convention of Cleveland, Tennessee, most earnestly request that you will offer special prayer for a revival of religion in all our different churches. We have a union prayer-meeting daily, and also public worship at night. We are earnestly laboring in the use of the means to secure the desired and promised blessing."

A clergyman said:

"We have heard requests read, and we have prayed. We have just sung

> "Amazing grace! how sweet the sound,
>   That saved a wretch like me;
> I once was lost, but now am found;
>   Was blind, but now I see.
>
> "'Twas grace that taught my heart to fear,
>   And grace my fears relieved;
> How precious did that grace appear
>   The hour I first believed."

He repeated these words with great emphasis and deep feeling, and continued:

"How many come here saying they cannot find the way to be saved—want to find it. O how slow to believe Him who has said, 'I am the Way, the Truth, and the Life.' O sinners, just believe this; you who are anxious, just believe these words of the blessed Jesus. He can give you day for night, and change your sorrow for everlasting songs. Jesus has done it all. He has borne your sins in His own body on the tree. He laid down His life for you. He rose from the dead for your justification. He has gone to be a priest forever for you. He is the great Mediator between God and man, and He lays His hand on both, that they may be reconciled.

"I believe there is a sympathy in spiritual anxiety and sorrow. I pity and pray for those who send these requests for prayer. Great is the mystery of godliness. We cannot reason, but we may believe."

A man arose in the back part of the room. He was a man in middle life, and apparently of more than ordinary intelligence. He said:

"I cannot fail to bear my humble testimony to the truths which have been repeated here. I have been coming here for some time. For a few days I have felt that I was born again—begotten anew in Christ Jesus. Some who hear me will be astonished to hear me say it. They know that I have been proud in saying that I would not believe what I could not understand. But I am free to say I cannot understand how God could have mercy on a wretch like me. But wretch as I was, Jesus has spoken peace to me. It was surprising grace. I want to say to all anxious ones here and everywhere, make but trial of His grace and love, and see how precious He is. O so precious."

The Revival of 1872 has now gone into history, but we shall hear good tidings of the outpouring of the Holy Spirit. Most earnest prayers have been offered in the meeting that God would everywhere revive His work.

News of revivals of religion came in from all quarters until it was believed that a larger number of revivals followed the "Week of Prayer" than have been since the great revival of 1858, and that a greater number have been added to the churches than any other since 1858, when the whole land was moved with the power of the Spirit.

THE END.

THE
Theological and Philosophical Library.

A Series of Text-Books, Original and Translated, for Colleges and Theological Seminaries.

EDITED BY

HENRY B. SMITH, D.D., and PHILIP SCHAFF, D.D.,

PROFESSORS IN THE UNION THEOLOGICAL SEMINARY, NEW YORK.

Messrs. Scribner, Armstrong & Co. propose to publish a select and compact Library of Text-Books upon all the main departments of Theology and Philosophy, adapted to the wants especially of ministers and students in all denominations.

Some of the works will be translated from the German and other languages; others will be based upon treatises by various authors; some will be written for the library by English or American scholars. The aim will be to furnish at least one condensed standard work on each of the scientific divisions of Theology and Philosophy, giving the results of the best critical investigations, excluding, however, such histories and commentaries as extend through many volumes.

The Initial Volume of this Series is Now Ready, viz.:

A HISTORY OF PHILOSOPHY,
FROM THALES TO THE PRESENT TIME.

By Dr. F. UEBERWEG, late Professor of Philosophy in the University of König_berg.

LANGE'S COMMENTARY.
ANOTHER OLD TESTAMENT VOLUME.
FIRST AND SECOND KINGS.

Translated and Edited by E. HARWOOD, D.D., *of New Haven, and* Rev. W. G. SUMNER, *of Morristown, N. J.*

One vol. 8vo, cloth..$5.00

The Volumes previously published are:

OLD TESTAMENT.—I. GENESIS. II. JOSHUA, JUDGES, and RUTH. III. PROVERBS, SONG OF SOLOMON, ECCLESIASTES. IV. JEREMIAH and LAMENTATION.

NEW TESTAMENT.—I. MATTHEW. II. MARK and LUKE. III. JOHN. IV. ACTS. V. THE EPISTLE OF PAUL TO THE ROMANS. VI. CORINTHIANS. VII. GALATIANS, EPHESIANS, PHILIPPIANS, COLOSSIANS. VIII. THESSALONIANS, TIMOTHY, TITUS, PHILEMON, and HEBREWS. IX. THE EPISTLES GENERAL OF JAMES, PETER, JOHN, and JUDE.

Each one vol. 8vo. Price per vol., in half calf, $7.50; in sheep, $6.50; in cloth, $5.00.

These works sent, post-paid, on receipt of the price, by

SCRIBNER, ARMSTRONG & CO. 654 Broadway N.Y

SYSTEMATIC THEOLOGY.

By CHARLES HODGE, D.D., of Princeton Theological Seminary.

Complete in three volumes 8vo. Tinted paper. Price per volume, in cloth, $4.50.

In these volumes are comprised the results of the life-long labors and investigations of one of the ablest theologians of the age. The work covers the ground usually occupied by treatises on Systematic Theology, and adopts the commonly received divisions of the subject: Theology (Vol. I.), Anthropology (Vol. II.), Soteriology and Eschatology (Vol. III.).

The various topics ranged under these different divisions are discussed with that close and keen analytical and logical power, combined with that simplicity, lucidity, and strength of style, which have already given Dr. Hodge a world-wide reputation as a controversialist and writer, and as an investigator of the great theological problems of the day.

THE SPEAKER'S COMMENTARY.

THE FIRST VOLUME OF

THE BIBLE COMMENTARY.

(Popularly known in England as "The Speaker's Commentary.")

THE PENTATEUCH:

Comprising Genesis, Exodus, Leviticus, Numbers, Deuteronomy.

Edited by Rev. HAROLD E. BROWNE, Author of "*Exposition of the Thirty-nine Articles;*" Rev. F. C. COOK, M.A., Canon of Exeter and General Editor of the "Bible Commentary;" Rev. SAM'L CLARK, M.A., and Rev. T. E. ESPIN, B.D., Warden of Queen's College, Birmingham.

1 vol. royal 8vo, 1,000 pages, with occasional illustrations, handsomely bound in extra brown cloth, with black and gilt lines. Per vol., $5.00.

This great work, which has been prepared by a combination of all the leading divines of the Church of England, had its origin in the widely-felt want of a plain explanatory Commentary on the Holy Scriptures, which should be at once more comprehensive and compact than any previously published. The cordial and enthusiastic reception which has been extended to the work, and the praise bestowed upon the first volume in England—even by those whose connections would lead them to the most severe and indeed hostile criticism—demonstrate the great success which the enterprise has already achieved. From the fulness, fairness, thoroughness, and candor with which all difficult questions are discussed, the Bible Commentary is sure to be satisfactory to the scholar; while the plain, direct, and devout manner in which the meaning of the Sacred Text is explained, thoroughly adapt it for the widest popular use, whether in the closet, in the family, or in the Sunday-school.

N.B.—*A full prospectus of the Bible Commentary sent to any address on application. Each volume of the Bible Commentary will be complete in itself, and may be purchased separately.*

These works sent, post-paid, on receipt of the price, by

SCRIBNER, ARMSTRONG & CO., 654 Broadway, N.Y.